BE
STRONG,
BE
WISE

Advance Praise

"In our post #MeToo world, where discussing sexual assault is finally acceptable and information is increasingly available, *Be Strong, Be Wise* paves the way for a new conversation by helping the reader ask the essential question, "What does sexual assault mean to *me*?" Interweaving real-life vignettes and sobering statistics within the context of our current social and political environment, Carpenter dives deep and helps create a personal connection to the complex layers related to all aspects of sexual assault. As a college professor, I highly recommend this book – you won't just learn something new about sexual assault, you'll learn something new about yourself."

– **Cathleen Ferrick**, college professor and parent

"As a college student, the fear of sexual assault is real. In a society where sexual violence seems almost "normal," Carpenter offers us a place to go from being afraid, to being aware. She brings us to an understanding that these attacks are anything but normal and gives us the tools to prevent them. *Be Strong, Be Wise* is eye-opening, relatable and empowering."

– **Crystal Baughman**, college student

"*Be Strong, Be Wise* has given me a type of third eye I never knew existed. I am more aware than I've ever been of my own being, my surroundings, and my safety. The set of "tools" that Amy Carpenter lays out for her readers have helped me to improve my own confidence and remind me that I can be a strong woman in a man's world. As a college student and aspiring writer, I found this book inspiring, beautifully written, and thoughtfully presented to young adults of any gender. Now that I've read this book, I feel more equipped than ever to tackle this world without doubting my worth, power, and ability to say "no". It also gives me hope for the next generation of students who will get to use these tools and, hopefully, create a new era of equality."

– **Mary Carlson Wanjiru**, college student and blogger

"As a college instructor, I interact with young people every day who are hungry to discuss the complexities of sexual assault, yet don't know where to begin. *Be Strong, Be Wise* opens the door to practical and inspiring conversation about sex, friendship, crossing the line, and how to advocate for yourself and your friends. Every young person should read this book before setting foot on a college campus."

– **Amy Amoroso**, college instructor and parent

"I wish that I had been fortunate enough to have a resource like *Be Strong, Be Wise* when I was in my teens and twenties. It is a short, easy-to-read, non-preachy, and highly informative tool kit for protecting oneself against sexual assault. I am tempted to leave a copy or two in every cafe or club that I know young women and men frequent, or stuff a copy in a family member's or friend's suitcase for college. Sexual assault can mark someone for a lifetime. One can be lucky or be prepared in their efforts to avoid that trauma. Be prepared with this book."

– **Rita Saliba**, lawyer, writer and parent

"As a college counselor, I found Amy Carpenter's book provided helpful and essential steps for navigating our rough cultural waters. Stories and statistics demonstrate the vulnerability of college girls today. This book pictures the safe passage to stronger, healthier, beautiful selves. A skilled therapist (who has taught this subject in high school) the author draws on her own story, along with the experiences of her many clients, and careful study, to provide what most of today's media miss. Beyond the reports of sensational news, distress and complicated litigation, she offers practical help for young women, men and the LGBTQ community in facing themselves, supporting their friends, and dealing with the enticing digital world. *Be Strong, Be Wise* is a must read for students, parents, clergy and educators."

– **Gail Borgman**, college counselor and parent

"*Be Strong, Be Wise* talks to youth in stunningly obvious truths about how we all contribute to an unsafe society and how we might begin to change these patterns. Clear, concise intelligence cuts to the quick with real stories as testament to how easily people of any gender become sexually damaged goods in plain open sight. Amy Carpenter's accumulated wisdom from twenty-five years as a psychotherapist clusters forthright questions for her readers to consider, reflect upon, and in answering, grow their street smarts. Well researched, it's a must-have survival guide for young people of all ages!"

               – **Kate Campbell**, teacher, artist, and parent

"As a psychologist and mother of two teenage boys about to leave for college, *Be Strong, Be Wise* is an invaluable resource to help young women and men navigate the complexities of social and sexual situations in order to prevent and protect themselves from unwanted sexual assault. It is written in clear, straight-forward language that interweaves real life vignettes, statistical data, concrete strategies, thought-provoking questions, practical guidance, and vital resources that make this book a must read. It will absolutely better anyone, young or old, in knowing how to keep themselves safe."

               – **Dr. Nina Silberman**, psychologist and parent

"*Be Strong, Be Wise* completely removes the stigma around opening a dialogue about sexual safety. The book champions personal empowerment and presents practical tools to employ safe habits when in social situations, as well as in personal and intimate relationships. Amy Carpenter's writing has a friendly, candid tone and she uses relatable examples of real-life social situations coupled with thought-provoking questions. As she states: 'The point is to be aware not afraid.' In no way does the book discourage the reader from making the most of college and having a good time. As the father of two young men, ages sixteen and eighteen, I found the information in the book invaluable as I anticipate my sons heading off on their own, not only with regard to college situations, but as they enter into a life outside their home for the first time. *Be Strong, Be Wise* is now required reading in my house, as it should be wherever young people reside."

– **Thomas Downey**, actor and parent

"Being a school counselor and a mother of two college-aged women, I found this book worth its weight in gold! Amy Carpenter has eloquently presented a topic that is pervasive and complicated. By connecting directly with her audience in a relaxed and familiar manner, Carpenter has created a clear pathway to accessing personal strength and wisdom, giving the reader power to make decisive choices in messy situations.

This book is an invaluable resource for all."

– **Jenny Roberts,** school counselor and parent

"*Be Strong, Be Wise* is a valuable guidebook for students that addresses sexual assault in a way that makes a difference. With twenty-five years as a psychotherapist and having personal experience with trauma, Ms. Carpenter offers easy, precise, and to-the-point prevention tips that help keep young people safe. As a teacher, I recommend this book to both students and educators. It offers to meet students where they are at, helping them to become informed rather than live in fear."

– **Josephine Grace**, teacher, author, and speaker

"It is refreshing to read a book that talks honestly and directly to young adults and teenagers about how to navigate social and sexual situations. Ms. Carpenter does this without undermining their savvy and intelligence by combining personal stories with statistical data. What she reveals and offers is concrete solutions to some of the toughest situations young people face, daily. The thoughtful and inquisitive questions she asks the reader throughout the book can help young adults begin, and continue to have, thoughtful conversations about their sexual/social lives."

– **Carol Morrisson**, artist and parent

"*Be Strong, Be Wise* is an important book for the #MeToo era. While Carpenter has written this manual for college students, every person can benefit from the examples, tools, and strategies she lays out. This guide to sexual safety is a quick read that first focuses on knowing who you are and how you react in tense situations. It then suggests what you can do to keep yourself and your friends safe. She also tackles what to do if an assault occurs. *Be Strong, Be Wise* is a fabulous resource and well-worth the read."

– **Gro Flatebo**, writer and parent

"*Be Strong, Be Wise* is an empowering and insightful read. This book should be a must for every young person getting ready to go out on their own. It explains in relatable terms how both women and men can protect themselves from unwanted and unwarranted sexual advances. The real-life stories are compelling and remind us that anyone can be in a vulnerable situation, but how it is handled at the time can avoid an uncomfortable and even more serious outcome. Ms. Carpenter has included well-written solutions that remind us that it is best to be proactive rather than reactive in preventing sexual assault. This book is an eye-opener and should be read by all; young and old."

– **Shelia Craig Whiteman**, teacher, speaker and parent

BE
STRONG,
BE
WISE

THE YOUNG ADULT'S GUIDE TO SEXUAL ASSAULT AWARENESS AND PERSONAL SAFETY

AMY R. CARPENTER

NEW YORK

LONDON • NASHVILLE • MELBOURNE • VANCOUVER

BE STRONG, BE WISE
The Young Adult's Guide to Sexual Assault
Awareness and Personal Safety

Published in New York, New York, by Morgan James Publishing in partnership with Difference Press. Morgan James is a trademark of Morgan James, LLC. www.MorganJamesPublishing.com

ISBN 9781631950872 paperback
ISBN 9781631950889 eBook
Library of Congress Control Number: 2020934157

Cover Design Concept: Jennifer Stimson

Editor: Emily Tuttle

Book Coaching: The Author Incubator

Author Photo: Crystal Brooke Photo

Cover Design by: Chris Treccani, 3dogcreative.net

Interior Design by: Melissa Farr, melissa@backporchcreative.com

Disclaimer

The tools discussed in this book apply to any young adult, whether they are in college or not. The principles, when used consistently, will decrease the likelihood of being victim to sexual assault—but they're meant as a guide, not a guarantee. I came up with the framework through my experience as a trauma clinician, youth worker, survivor, and parent. Still, there are far too many ways assault can happen to speak about them all in one book. My focus here is based on the stories I've heard through my role as a therapist, stories that have led me to understand sexual assault is more preventable than we've yet acknowledged. This book offers a pathway toward the kind of individual and social empowerment that decreases risk.

Morgan James is a proud partner of Habitat for Humanity Peninsula and Greater Williamsburg. Partners in building since 2006.

Get involved today! Visit
MorganJamesPublishing.com/giving-back

To #MeToo and all social change movements
that call on us to remember our dignity.

Table of Contents

Author's Note: How to Approach This Book

Since more readers mean more people using safety measures, I knew if I came across as boring in writing this book, I'd lose those who might be on the fence about reading a sexual safety guide. So, my goals were in conflict. How could I inform the reader without boring them? How could I help them integrate the tools without sounding like a textbook or manual? In the end, I decided to go with my gut and trust that the average eighteen-plus-year-old person is able to grasp several concepts simultaneously, as well as apply them to their own life (albeit, with some help.) In this way, I deliver the material as directly as possible, giving the reader all the information they need to know without using a lot of unnecessary descriptions or clinical mumbo-jumbo. Also, the topic is not a light one, but there is a way of talking about it in a light manner.

Chapters 1 through 3 set the backdrop, providing information to readers of any age, but by Chapter 4, the narrative voice changes and is directed solely to young adults. In conversational style, I address the reader as "you" through the remainder of the book.

To write about the experience of the average young person when it comes to intimate relationships is like trying to identify a favorite movie, which is to say, impossible. In Chapter 7, when I discuss sex and dating, I opted for minor graphic descriptions to get the necessary points across. There are readers who may find these too graphic or, conversely, too innocent. If the tools are accessible, it does not matter. Additionally, the accounts of sexual assault are written sparsely for the most part. This is out of respect for the contributors' stories. They are not mine, and certain details aren't necessary to a discussion on safety. In order to ensure privacy, all the contributors' names have been changed.

The questions at the end of each chapter help integrate the information and make it more usable, which means the wisdom available is determined by what the reader brings to it.

Lastly, since women are far more likely to be victims of assault, I discuss sexism as a primary risk force, along with homophobia and transphobia. That said, the guidelines here are written for both men and women. The pronouns "he/she" are used primarily throughout the book, and when discussing the gender-fluid community, the pronoun "they" is used exclusively.

CHAPTER 1

The Making of a Movement

Most young adults don't think sexual assault will happen to them. They might feel they're too well-supported, too smart, too sheltered, or too worldly to ever become a victim. And yet, according to the Rape, Abuse, and Incest National Network (RAINN), there's a sexual assault approximately every ninety-two seconds in the US, with more than half involving victims between the ages of eighteen and thirty-four.

Perhaps the most unresolved issue of our time, sexual assault—classified as "unwanted sexual touch"—is also a taboo subject. Victims often choose secrecy; in fact, according to RAINN's reports, out of 1,000 sexual assault cases, only five offenders will serve jail time. As a psychotherapist, I've treated sexual trauma for nearly twenty-five years, and I've never gotten used to hearing the troubling stories my clients have shared. When the #MeToo movement came along, so did the realization that I'd spent enough time in my career responding to assault, and perhaps it was time to work on preventing it.

The #MeToo movement helped us break down walls of secrecy by creating an arena where survivors could share their stories in the form of two simple words: me too. Now it's time to create a new movement focused on keeping young people safe.

Another Kind of College Prep

When I taught sexual assault prevention classes at a local high school, the students knew how to respond to the "what-if" scenarios that took place in familiar territory, like school. For example, when discussing whether it was okay for a coach to slap an athlete on the butt as they were heading onto the field, the responses were mixed but immediate. Many of the young men answered in the affirmative, while the young women answered with a concrete "no." We explored gender differences and the definition of assault as it applied to sports in the lively conversation that followed.

When we talked about life after high school, the reactions grew vague. To their credit, why should the average eighteen-year-old apprehend, let alone understand, something they have not yet experienced, especially when experience is how we learn? Yet often that is what parents, teachers, and young people expect. Somehow, through trial and error, osmosis, or a keen gut instinct, college-age adults will go off into the world and just *figure it out*.

I liken this to travel. Before visiting India, I read every guidebook I could get my hands on, watched documentaries, and played twenty questions with anyone who had been to that immense country. Still, nothing could have prepared me for the teeming, electric, and sometimes overwhelming reality of India. Life after high school can feel much the same; like something altogether different, because it is.

No matter how independent or savvy a young person may be or how many adventures they experienced, life after the age of eighteen is a whole different ball game—a new playing field, new rules, new teammates, new learning habits. While their mentors in high school, whether a coach, a parent, or a teacher, were apt to say what was expected on any given day, after high school, young adults are on their own as both coach and team member. The good news is this can be one of the most exciting stages we get in a lifetime.

The average college freshman is no slouch and usually far more aware than most adults give them credit for. However, the #MeToo movement has taught us a few truths that can't be ignored because they affect how to play the game of adulthood. Although these truths were around long before #MeToo, the movement helped bring them forward into a whole new light. Here are a few of the biggies:

————————————— # —————————————

1. If you are female, there's a twenty-five percent chance you will experience sexual assault before

you graduate college or have been in the workforce for four years (rainn.org).

2. If you are male, you are not guaranteed safety, since seventeen percent of reported sexual assaults occur against men.

3. If you are a member of the LGBTQ or gender-fluid community, the rates are even higher, with studies suggesting that approximately half of transgender people and bisexual women will experience sexual violence at some point in their lifetimes. According to the Centers for Disease Control and Prevention, forty percent of gay men have experienced sexual violence other than rape, compared to twenty-one percent of heterosexual men.

———————————— # ————————————

All of these stats are even more troubling when we consider that the ACLU has estimated ninety-five percent of rapes on college campuses go unreported. Now we have a generation of college students who should be overjoyed at the prospect of independence but instead many are expressing fear. On June 8, 2016, Terrin Waack, a Sporting News intern and a student at the University of Alabama wrote an article titled: "As a College Student, I Live in Fear of Sexual Assault."

In it, she writes, "I'm scared because I'm surrounded by stories of rape and sexual assault, so much so they're becoming a norm. When another instance arises, it's no longer shocking. It's almost expected: Who's next?"

Terrin's words echo the thoughts of many college students, especially women. Yet aside from whether or not to carry mace, the prevention terms we use haven't strayed far from "stranger danger" and "good touch, bad touch," terms children learn as early as pre-school. The statistics indicate that victims most often know the offenders, so avoiding strangers doesn't guarantee safety, and what we learned from #MeToo is that many reported incidents occurred with offenders in positions of power. So how do we keep people safe if such child-like terms are applied to something much more nuanced and complex? Exploring the history of #MeToo begins to provide an answer.

The Movement That Changed the World

On October 15, 2017, at approximately nine p.m., actress Alyssa Milano was snuggling in bed with her daughter Bella when she was overcome by what she later described as a "mommy moment." She found herself praying to God that her daughter would never have to endure the sexually traumatic experiences she went through when she was younger. Without thinking much about it, Milano sent out a short message from her phone, asking that if anyone had ever experienced assault or harassment, they tweet back "#MeToo." Within seven hours, she received 35,000 responses. Within twenty-four hours, the number leapt to twelve million, and forty-eight hours later, the tweet had reached eighty-two countries.

A global movement was born.

The concerns around sexual violence in the US had been building for years prior to Milano's tweet as more executives and people in power were named as offenders. The phrase "Me Too" had been around for a while as well. Tarana Burke, activist and founder of "Just Be Inc.," an organization serving sexual assault survivors, first used the term in 2006 in order to promote "empowerment through empathy" among women of color who were assault survivors. Burke originally identified the term when she witnessed a thirteen-year-old abuse survivor describe her experience. "I didn't have a response or a way to help her in that moment, and I couldn't even say 'me too,'" Burke later told the *New York Times*.

There's a reason why it took a movement for the world to sit up and notice how big the problem is. In fact, in her interview with the *New York Times*, Tarana Burke described sexual assault as an "epidemic" in the United States.

As we'll discuss in this book, victim-blaming can happen in a myriad of ways and can have massive implications on reporting outcomes. If someone has been assaulted and is then brave enough to share their story, you can bet they might regret coming forward if they are then ridiculed or ostracized by their peers. As traumatic as victim-blaming is, #MeToo widened the doorway for people to share their experience in a way that allows them to feel supported, rather than rejected. Now we can talk more openly about the problem and how to address it in a way that makes a difference.

What is Sexual Assault?

In order to have an effective conversation about prevention, we first need to understand the exact definition of the problem. Usually, people are pretty blown away by just how broad it is:

"Sexual assault is commonly recognized as any unwanted sexual contact or threats of sexual contact. Sexual assault includes the touching of another person's body in a sexual manner without that person's express consent, even if the touching occurs through clothing. This sexual assault definition also includes kissing, groping, and fondling.

"The term 'express consent' refers to an individual's clearly stated and voluntary expression of choice in any matter. Any person who is incapacitated, whether by physical or psychological ailment, or by drugs or alcohol, or who is under the age of majority, *cannot* legally consent to sexual contact. Therefore, sexual touching, or sexual acts performed on such an individual, are considered sexual assault, regardless of the perpetrator's claim that the victim consented (Legal Dictionary)."

Sexual harassment is defined as "behavior characterized by the making of unwelcome and inappropriate sexual remarks or physical advances in a workplace or other professional or social situation."

Let's think about the slap on the butt a coach gives an athlete as they run onto the field. To some, this is a normal facet of being on a team and is no big deal. To others, such an act could be as inappropriate as a slap on the face. It all depends on prior life experience and the way that touch gets expressed on a daily basis. If someone has been victim to prior assault, a slap on the butt is likely to be re-traumatizing.

In understanding the definition of assault, a keyword looms large: *unwanted*. This is where self-awareness and communication become the most effective safety tools in our arsenal. While many forms of touch, such as a slap on the butt, might seem harmless, no one has the right to cross our physical boundaries without permission. It can be hard to conceptualize at first, but a kiss on the cheek, if unwanted, is still assault.

A long-established relationship between friends or family members implies permission, but even in these cases, there are appropriate and inappropriate examples of physical affection. A good way of defining the difference is to know how it *feels* to receive the advance. This helps build awareness of personal limits when it comes to physical contact. There may be no wrong intention in such displays of affection, but even with family members, it's important to know what is comfortable versus what isn't *and to communicate that clearly.*

When interviewed by the Associated Press a year after her original tweet, Alyssa Milano declared, "Any time we are able to discuss things, we de-mystify them and make them more tangible to overcome."

Here's a way to begin discussing what sexual assault and harassment mean to you. Try answering the following questions from two different standpoints: first, according to the definition of assault, and then, according to *you.* Your answers will help build inner wisdom around the deeper meaning of "good touch, bad touch."

——————————— # ———————————

Written Exercise: Is It or Is It Not Sexual Assault When...

1. A coach slaps one of his female players on the butt as she walks past to go on the field.

2. A female tutor arrives for her session with a male student and suddenly gives him a hug and a kiss on the cheek as she comes through the door.

3. A group of students from an opposing team yells obscenities at a female goalie, and one of them threatens her sexually if she keeps the other team from scoring.

4. A young woman gets drunk at a party and a male friend (also drunk) grabs her breast as she walks by.

5. A group of students at a party is playing spin the bottle. One guy in the group tells his friends he's tired and doesn't feel like playing. The rest of the group call him a baby and threaten to tell the whole school what a baby he is if he doesn't play.

6. A town librarian is helping a gender-fluid college student locate a book for a research project. At one point, the librarian tells them how handsome they are, touches their hair and says, "There are books I could show you that are a lot sexier than this."

7. A group of college freshmen is at a pool party. One of the young men has had a lot to drink and begins making sexual comments to the women. Suddenly, he pulls his bathing suit down and flashes his genitals at them.

8. Mike, an eighteen-year-old high school senior, has a crush on his male youth group leader, who is twenty-three. The youth group leader drives Mike home one day and tells Mike he would like to kiss him. Mike agrees.

----------------------------- # -----------------------------

Now, take another quick look; do any of these examples qualify as harassment? If so, which ones?

When you're finished, check out your answers. In terms of which scenarios qualify as harassment, if you answered with something like, "They all do," then you are on the right track! The scenarios described in questions one, two, four, five and six could all be classified as sexual assault, since they involve *unwanted sexual touch*. The scenarios offered in questions three and seven would also classify, since the offenders *made sexual threats* (to the goalie and to the group of women at the pool party.) In question eight, although Mike is eighteen, his youth group leader's role creates a power differential in their relationship. Though Mike consented to the kiss, the youth leader overstepped the boundary of that role, classifying his action as sexual assault.

CHAPTER 2

Following the Signs

Rebecca had been coming to my therapy office for more than a year when #MeToo started, and it took almost as long for her to feel ready to share her story. The effects of sexual assault had left long-lasting scars that no one in Rebecca's life knew about though they affected her every day. #MeToo had given her hope but was perplexing as well. How could we have let things get this far, and what happens now? Rebecca's response was not dissimilar from those of my other clients who had assault histories.

When the Kavanaugh hearing took place on the heels of #MeToo, I saw the hope that had been building in many of my clients get crushed. Rebecca, who was sexually assaulted by an upper classman when she was a freshman in high school, and then assaulted again at ages sixteen and eighteen, told me she tried to watch every minute of the hearing.

"How could they not believe her?" Rebecca asked in tears at her next session, referencing Christine Blasey-Ford's brave and articulate testimony of sexual assault at the hands of Brett Kavanaugh in 1982 when Christine was still in high school.

Rebecca was not alone. Several others came to therapy that week stunned and dismayed at the outcome that sent Brett Kavanaugh to his seat as a Supreme Court justice. While at the time, there may have been assault survivors who did *not* have that reaction to the hearing, I wasn't working with any of them. As a clinician, my mind reeled with how best to respond to Rebecca and others who were visibly shaken. What I hoped to do was point them in some kind of direction. "Here!" I wanted to say. "Here's a road map, a way out of your grief." Searching for advice, I called our local sexual assault response organization, and learned they had been flooded with five times their usual call volume the week of the hearing. The woman I spoke with offered helpful feedback, but in the end, I realized the most important thing I could offer was a safe, accepting space where my clients could process what was happening in national news and how these larger stories affected their own personal stories.

At around that time, I started to get a familiar *I'm going to have to write about this* feeling. For as long as I could hold a pencil, writing has been a way to process life, and I had something in me I needed to say. The article I began working on was about sexual assault and its effect on the developing identity. Since most assaults happen in young adulthood, I had worked with countless people still haunted by the memories, triggers, and patterns in their life that they knew held them back.

The title of the piece was, "The Invisible Master of Ceremonies: Sexual Assault and the Shaping of Identity." The article felt powerful to me, and when I presented it to my writers' group, they concluded it was good—well-written, well-researched, and impactful. But where would I submit it? To other therapists who could say the same thing based on their own observations in trauma treatment? To scientific journals where the medical and psychological community may or may not get a hold of it, reading it from the standpoint of science or practice methodology? All of that seemed empty to me, so I did what any well-meaning writer would do. I shelved the article until I could gain traction on some path that felt like I was helping people instead of adding more noise to an already well-populated space.

Then something horrible happened. Someone close to me, who attends school with my daughter and who I'll call Lily, was sexually assaulted while volunteering at a church soup kitchen with the National Honor Society. It was one of three known assaults that took place at the school over the span of a year.

Lily is a go-getter, an A student, star athlete, and high-level performer on every front, yet she was harmed in the community she grew up in. On the day of the assault, she was with a group of twenty-six peers. Her teachers were nearby, as well as a supervising priest and nearly fifty soup kitchen attendees. Still, the perpetrator found a way to gain access to Lily and lure her into a private room where he touched her inappropriately and kissed her on the mouth. As a parent, I had always lived in fear that my daughter might one day be assaulted. Knowing too many horror stories from my professional life made me concerned for her well-being many of the times she wasn't with me. After what Lily went through, I realized parents are never guaranteed their kids' safety. We can do our best to protect them, but we also need to teach them how to best protect themselves.

The police intervened in Lily's behalf and the church and school were held accountable, but on multiple levels, Lily's assault was *preventable*. I realized I'd been approaching the problem from only one angle. Psychotherapists and trauma experts have more information than ever before on how to respond to assault. What we don't have is a book on prevention that provides explicit information about sexual safety. College campuses and police departments put out bullet-point safety tips, and there are a few articles online, but in my search thus far, nothing in the available literature is comprehensive. Nothing speaks to young people where they are at.

With a small sense of horror, it dawned on me that part of the reason assaults are so common is because they've become, in some ways, *normal*. I even had a friend of mine say to me, after telling her that I was thinking about writing a book on sexual assault prevention, "But doesn't that just happen at some point in college, no matter what you say or do to try to stop it?" The statement probably reflects how a lot of people feel.

I had my work cut out for me, and at first, felt out of my depth. Who am I to talk about sexual assault prevention? I'm a clinician, not an activist or policymaker. How could I discuss with expertise, a topic as broad and impactful as this? Then I remembered my early days in child welfare, where I was first introduced to trauma and recovery, and how in graduate school I elected (among few others) to study sexual abuse treatment for my final clinical thesis. After getting my license and working as a school-based counselor, I helped organize groups for at-risk girls and gave lectures on female empowerment at several young adult conferences.

Still, more than all the training, classes, and years spent working in clinical practice, I also had my own assault story. Maybe this story was the reason I spent twenty-five years treating trauma. Developing the pieces of this book helped me better formulate the pieces of my journey, and I could finally see how it all fit.

I was eight years old, living in Trenton, New Jersey, when the attack took place in a field bordering my back yard. Ten neighborhood boys came onto the property when my parents weren't home. They stripped me from the waist down and held me, screaming and frantically trying to free myself, as one of them took his penis out and the rest of them yelled for him to "Stick it in her!" The boy was my age, though most of the others were significantly older. Child testosterone levels prevented him from doing much more than stand there, perhaps nearly as frightened as I was, with pre-pubescent genitalia hanging uselessly above his folded-down pants. Fortunately, none of the others took his place. After a few horrible minutes, screaming louder than I've ever screamed, the boys all decided it "wasn't worth it" and let me go. It turned out that gang of bullies had their limits, and one of them was rape. They were violent enough to terrorize me but didn't violate me in a way that would be more physically and psychologically damaging. In some respects, I got lucky.

Due to embarrassment, I never told anyone about that afternoon until I was in my mid-twenties. When I shared the story with my parents, they were horrified, blamed themselves, and tried to talk it through with me, but the emotional effects were a mystery. I had always been afraid when walking down a dark street alone, but wasn't any woman? I knew that crowded buses and night clubs were places one might get grabbed or fondled, but didn't everyone? The anxiety I experienced so often living in the city, even if it was just being alone at night in my apartment was, to me, normal and a necessary part of being female.

Later, every therapist I worked with told me that what happened in the field was an act of sexual violence that had likely informed my way of handling myself in the world. All I knew was that I had never been so afraid in my life. It wasn't until much later that I realized the low-grade panic I sometimes felt might not happen for everyone. Being more aware of where that feeling comes from, I've done enough healing work to gently talk myself through it. Even so, there's one effect that my psyche will not relinquish. To this day, if anyone grabs my arm or wrist, even in play, I am once again pinned to the ground in that field, and all my body knows is terror. My autonomic nervous system, otherwise known as the trauma brain, doesn't register the difference between an act of kindness or an act of violence when it comes to someone grabbing my wrist, and I can get downright vicious in defending myself.

A high percentage of sexual assault victims feel uncomfortable sharing their story due to intense shame. Like myself, many people who endure sexual trauma don't realize at first the impact it has on their lives. In the wake of #MeToo, we now have the opportunity to make space for these stories and the sharing of truth that allows for greater healing.

In her famous TED talk, "The Power of Vulnerability," international speaker Brené Brown said that shame is the thing "no one wants to talk about… and the less you talk about it, the more you have it." #MeToo invited victims of assault to step beyond their shame, the same way so many of my clients, like Rebecca, have done. When I told each of them I was writing a book on sexual assault prevention, they wanted to share their experiences so that young people could benefit. I owe these individuals a ton of gratitude for their bravery. We now know how big the problem is. This book offers a solution.

3 A View from the Ship's Bow

I was forty pages into my guidebook on sexual safety when people started telling me, "Young adults don't read that kind of stuff." By then, I'd spent months researching and drafting an easy-to-follow formula that I believed would work for any high school graduate (or non-graduate), regardless of location, maturity level, or life experience. There wasn't much that could deter me, but it was deflating to hear all that work could amount to nothing. The more I talked to people, the more I realized the college prep process is filled with *assumptions* that impact young adults in significant ways. Here are a few of them:

———————————— # ————————————

1. Young adults only care about their phones and their friends and don't have the attention span to read a book on safety.
2. Young people help each other stay safe and have their own ways of doing that as a group, so they don't need any more guidance.

3. High school teaches everything young people need to know about safety.

4. Assault only happens to people who don't have good boundaries.

5. Young people aren't capable of talking about things that make them uncomfortable, and sexual assault is scary and uncomfortable.

———————————— # ————————————

I could go on and on. It's easy to see that functioning with even one of these assumptions won't do anything to decrease risk. In continuing my project, I decided to adopt the attitude that young people are capable of more than these assumptions, but since we'd all rather talk about almost anything *but* assault prevention, assumptions dictate protocol. This is why parents, teachers, coaches, guidance counselors, and youth leaders struggle to discuss sexual safety. It makes *everyone* uncomfortable.

With the enactment of child safety laws, prevention education is now available in public schools, beginning in the early grades. However, by high school graduation, most of that information, if not reinstated for older age groups, has been forgotten or relegated to simplistic terms such as "stranger danger." The hard truth, and what is true in countless cases, is that often the outcome could have been different if a few action steps were taken, not just by the victim but also by anyone in proximity to the victim at the time of assault.

To be clear: *sexual assault is never anyone's fault but that of the offenders.* Still, there are behaviors and thought forms that increase personal safety and can be obtained easily without missing any fun or freedom. Fear is like an inflatable balloon—it can expand in a moment. In these pages, the reader will increase their safety odds by becoming informed rather than afraid, since empowerment goes a lot farther than fear in lowering risk. The Be Strong, Be Wise framework is designed to build awareness for what each young person brings to the game of adulthood when it's played in a safety-minded way.

To the Reader

Imagine you're on a ship, destined to arrive on a distant island, and you're standing at the bow, binoculars in hand. When you look through the lens, you can view the whole island and its flora. You see a white sandy beach covered in rocks and shells and bordered by a sloping line of palm trees, but beyond that, the details aren't clear yet. As you get closer, you sharpen the lens to notice a beautiful conch shell sitting among the crystals of sand. There are hundreds of other shells and rocks on the beach, but this one is magnificent. You're determined to make it to the island so that you can find the shell, look at it up close, and listen to the oceanic sound it makes. First, you'll have to broaden the lens again in order to see just where on the beach the conch shell sits since you don't want to mistake it for another one when you arrive. That's the shell you want!

Strange as it may sound, this book functions the same way as your voyaging ship. In order to appreciate the beauty of the conch shell, it's important to notice the environment around it. The other shells, rocks, trees, and sand only help that unique shell to stand out from all the rest, because guess what? *You* are the magnificent conch shell. There may be many others on the beach, but none is as important and as perfect as you. So, the more you get to know the shell's surroundings, the more you're able to identify it among the rocks and shells nearby.

The same is true for your new safety protocol. In the next few chapters, we'll explore the "surroundings" of your conch shell by taking a broad-lens view of the life stage you're in and the forces that affect it, starting with *gender*. To appreciate the value of your shell, you'll want to know the factors that went into making it what it is. In Chapter 4, we'll look at some of the cultural imprints that affect men, women, and gender-fluid people. In Chapter 5, we'll narrow the lens to explore how these roles affect a crucial aspect of your conch's island: *friendships*.

By then, you are ready to land on the beach. You'll have built an awareness of the island and will be confident in knowing the environmental forces that affect your shell. In Chapter 6, you'll come to appreciate the shell's unique details by exploring the subject of *self-knowledge*, the most important safety tool we can possess.

We'll talk about how self-awareness and intuitive skill can be used in risky situations and how you can learn to trust your gut to keep yourself safe. After that, you're ready to put it to the test through our discussion of *dating life*.

In Chapter 7, we pull all the tools together in support of your romantic relationships. This is an especially beautiful part of your island when safety is in place. We'll discuss how social media can be used effectively and how to protect your boundaries when they're in danger of being crossed. By the end of the chapter, you'll have a deeper sense of what you bring to new relationships and how to make sure you're in a healthy one.

At the end of almost every chapter in this book, there are a series of questions. I know. You've had enough questions thrown at you in high school to last a lifetime, but these are designed to act as conversation points. Since discussing safety is difficult, the questions are like road signs to get you thinking, talking, and exploring what the answers mean to *you*. I also think you'll find them interesting.

Now, the hard fact is that there are people reading this book who have already experienced assault. In Chapter 8, we take a sensitive look at *sexual assault response*. It's never too late to respond, and it's never too late to talk about it, but sometimes the possibilities are overwhelming, and initially, it's hard to navigate them. In this chapter, you'll find all the information you'll need to feel supported in taking those first steps. We'll discuss the national and local organizations designed to respond, as well as ways to approach the subject with friends and family. There is no right or wrong path to sharing your experience, and by the end of the chapter, you'll know why it's important to talk about it and how to find the path that's best for you.

In Chapter 9, you'll integrate what you've learned by exploring the obstacles to safety protocol and how you can manage them. In closing, our final chapter will introduce the idea of what it means to be a "movement maker." You will be among the first to enter the workforce since #MeToo, which means you have the opportunity to share your wisdom with others and to be a voice for change—in other words, a movement maker. Just by being more self-aware, informed, and confident (which I guarantee you will be by the end of this book), you'll have the skills needed to support yourselves and others in living a freer life.

Are you ready? Let's take out those binoculars and check out your island. There may be some invisible forces to know about before breaking land...

The Roles We Play

Everyone knows that children tend to look to their parents for guidance, influence, and behavior modeling. However, by the age of seventeen, there's a lot less care about good ol' Mom and Dad and a lot more about the person sitting next to you in biology class. Erik Erikson, the famous developmental theorist, called this stage "intimacy versus isolation." Young adults are invested in discovering how to have intimate relationships (platonic and romantic) with people who are decidedly *not* family members. Self-understanding is therefore shaped primarily by what young adults see other young adults doing or not doing. The questions that come up along the way might look something like:

---------------- # ----------------

1. Do I want to try out for the tennis team even though my boyfriend says it's a lame sport?
2. Should I go on birth control since all my friends are, even though I am not currently sexually active?

3. Should I tell the dean of students that my TA made a crude sexual comment to me, even though my friends might find out and I'd be embarrassed?

———————————— # ————————————

These types of explorations are an aspect of what Erikson called the "individuation" process. Adults are wise to recognize it as a normal part of what young people do in order to decide what type of person they want to become. In this chapter, we'll discuss how that influence applies to gender roles (female, male, and gender fluid) and, in turn, safety.

Cultivating the Feminine Warrior

As we've discussed, the ACLU estimates that ninety-five percent of rapes on college campuses go unreported, and most of them are against women. This problem is affected, in part, by what I call the "good girl phenomenon," or the need to be liked. Learning to let go of this need is a necessary attitude adjustment in the fight for gender equality and increased safety for girls. It has taken many of us years, even decades, to release the deep cultural imprint around what it means to "be good." Thankfully, we are seeing another rise of feminine warrior energy in the wake of #MeToo. Still, the good girl that lives inside many of us will not go away quietly without resistance; there's just too much social conditioning that keeps her around. The only way to ask our inner good girl to take leave is to be aware of her voice when she shows up and examine whether her feedback is necessary. If not, there's a seat in the back row waiting for her.

To be clear: we love the good girl. Her presence is important and helpful in many situations. If two friends are in a fight and not talking, the good girl—who is friends with them both—might encourage peacetime by suggesting the arguing friends compromise with each other. The good girl tends to do well in school, is a model citizen, and is generally well-liked. Our inner good girl is probably amiable, sweet, and happy because *being* good *feels* good, for the most part. However, if the good girl is getting in the way of personal progress, self-expression, and most of all, *safety*, she needs to take a time-out and let the inner warrior run the show.

The good girl is also more likely to silently suffer than make waves in her social circle in a way that could render her an outcast, even if only in her mind. In a dangerous situation or on the heels of an assault, she may decide she'd "rather not" make a report to the authorities because there's just too much public shame and embarrassment. What she might not realize is that reporting goes a long way in decreasing the sense of victimhood and powerlessness that so often attend the aftermath of sexual assault.

It Was Nobody's Fault and Everybody's Fault

I'd like to go back to Lily's story. Being a strong and thoughtful person, Lily asked me to share it so that others can learn from her experience.

Lily was preparing for college when the story begins. A high school honor student, she was involved in her community in many positive ways. One of these centered around the National Honor Society (NHS) where students volunteered monthly at a local church soup kitchen, a service relationship that had been going on for twenty-five years.

A new priest had taken over the church when Lily started her volunteer duties alongside her fellow NHS students and two teachers who "staffed" the event. This priest, who we will call Rev. L., had an agenda she presented to the teachers and students. She told the group that they were "privileged rich kids" because they lived in a wealthier community than the attendees of the soup kitchen, many of whom were homeless or lived in poverty. Rev. L. indicated that it was the students' job to "bridge the gap" and "mingle" with the attendees so as to avoid "toxic charity," such as serving food without engaging in dialogue.

Now, Lily is a bona fide good girl. She's kind and thoughtful and eager to please the adults in her life who hold positions of authority. When Rev. L. instructed the students, something in Lily's gut told her that what the priest said wasn't right. Rev. L. had never met the NHS students before; how did she know they were privileged or rich? However, it wasn't in Lily to question the authority of an adult in charge, let alone a priest. So, when the soup kitchen commenced, Lily was the first to volunteer by sitting down with one of the attendees, an older man who appeared to be in his sixties.

Lily and the man spent an entire hour talking under Rev. L.'s supervision. The teachers, who felt pushed aside by the Rev., were in the kitchen attending to food prep. They assumed Rev. L. would take responsibility for the volunteers since she said she would oversee the first "mingle" session. Lily hadn't been taught that certain men and women have an agenda other than friendship when it comes to "mingling." The official name for this kind of agenda is called "grooming." What this older man was doing with Lily as they talked was "grooming" her to think of him as a kind, safe, and trustworthy person. He asked about her school activities, told her she was nice, and presented himself as nothing more than friendly. At the close of the soup kitchen, this man, who I will call "B," spontaneously embraced Lily in a hug and gave her a kiss on the cheek.

Is such a minor advance considered sexual assault? Absolutely.

Rev. L. observed the kiss and asked Lily if she was okay. Lily, unsure of herself and the nature of the unwanted touch, said, "I think so," and the matter was dropped. The teachers, who did not see the kiss, weren't told by Rev. L., nor was anyone made aware that a student was being groomed by one of the attendees. Lily, being the good girl, came home and told her mother that a "nice, older man" gave her a hug and kiss on the cheek. Her mother did the usual mother stuff—she asked Lily if she was okay, whether or not she felt safe, and whether the staff there handled the situation appropriately. Lily said yes to every question because Lily didn't know otherwise. Her mom assumed the matter was handled by the teachers and staff in charge, and again, the matter was dropped.

Fast forward a month, and the NHS students were back at soup kitchen volunteering. Only this time, Rev. L. was not there. The two teachers supervising the group assumed the students were still supposed to mingle and, given that they were short-staffed, split their time between the dining room and the kitchen. When "B" sought out Lily again, Lily willingly sat down with him, only this time she noticed his behavior was different. "B" told Lily what a pretty girl she was and that he wished he was "thirty years younger." He asked her if she had a boyfriend and at one point took hold of her hands. Lily tried not to respond to "B's" statements. Her friends nearby saw that she was uncomfortable but didn't intervene because they assumed Lily was doing what she was told—bridging the gap with soup kitchen guests.

At the close of the hour, one of the students fainted in the kitchen, and the teachers rushed to respond. That's when "B" made his move. He told Lily that he wanted to say goodbye to her in private and asked her to step into the hallway with him. Lily brought her phone, knowing that if she pressed the off button five times, the police would come. She went with "B" because she assumed, especially after Rev. L. admonished the students, that she should give him the benefit of the doubt. No one was assisting her, and she felt she had no recourse. When she stepped out into the hallway, "B" hugged her, and while hugging her, passed his hands over her buttocks. Lily pulled away, at which point "B" leaned in and kissed her on the mouth. Lily immediately walked back to the dining room as "B" said to her, "Don't tell anyone about this."

The good news is that Lily did the opposite of what "B" asked. She told her friends, who told her teachers, who then called her parents and the police. "B" was later arrested for sexual assault (kiss on the cheek and the mouth) and inappropriate sexual touching of a minor (placing his hands on her buttocks). Everyone, especially Lily, learned a difficult but important lesson that day, which is that no one, not even a priest, a parent, or a teacher, has the right to tell you how you should behave in a situation that involves risk.

The assault against Lily would have been prevented if *any* of the following had taken place:

———————— # ————————

1. Rev. L., instead of intimidating the students, taught them how to mingle with guests in an appropriate way (including avoiding sitting with one person for too long).

2. Her mother, instead of assuming the matter was handled by staff in charge, called the teachers to report, "My daughter told me she was kissed on the cheek by one of the attendees."

3. The teachers, instead of assuming Rev. L. was providing adequate supervision, kept closer watch of the students.

4. Lily's friends, when observing the grooming behavior, stepped in to say, "You look uncomfortable. Wanna take a bathroom break and check in with each other?"

5. Lily herself, instead of listening to the promptings of her inner good girl, had listened to her gut.

———————— # ————————

This story teaches us that being "good" should never override being safe. In the end, Lily learned that the most important relationship when it comes to avoiding risk, is her relationship with herself.

Thanks to Lily's determination, good things came from her bad experience. Lily's school administration took a closer look at their volunteer programs and realized they had a lot of service projects where students were only minimally supervised. The system was immediately restructured so that what Lily experienced could be avoided in the future. Likewise, Lily's mother filed a complaint with the church diocese. It turned out the whole church system was functioning much the same way that Rev. L.'s church was, which meant that volunteers were not being fully protected. Rev. L. was required to go through appropriate safety training while the diocese took a state-wide look at how to ensure a safety-first agenda for soup kitchens. Lily went on to help organize a safety forum at her school so that other students could learn about prevention protocol and how to stick up for themselves in risky situations. Lily discovered she had an inner warrior all along, and that warrior was capable of manifesting some powerful things for the sake of positive change.

Lily asked me to share her story so that readers can look at community involvement from a new angle. There's no reason anyone should be afraid to get involved in the public sector through activism and service work. These are some of the most gratifying outlets we have in life, and they bring a great deal of good to our wider communities and world. However, they can involve variables that are hard to predict, which means being safety-minded should be first on our to-do list.

If you are in a volunteer capacity, know who's in charge, and listen to your gut on the safety protocols in place. If it seems the system is functioning in sloppy fashion, say something. If you feel uncomfortable with what you're being asked to do, don't hesitate to stick up for yourself. Work with your team, and check in with each other along the way. If someone looks like they may be in a compromising situation, stepping in with a friendly, "Hey, how are you doing?" can neutralize the scenario immediately.

Meanwhile, here are some questions to ask your inner good girl:

———————————— # ————————————

1. How many times in the past week have you known the answer in a class discussion but did not raise your hand because it would draw attention to yourself?
2. How many times a day do you say you're "sorry?"
3. How often, when you disagree with someone, do you keep your feelings to yourself in order to avoid conflict?
4. How often do you steer clear of a political debate with someone who thinks differently than you?
5. How often have you decided against joining a public protest even though you agree with the cause?

———————————— # ————————————

Check out your answers and give it some thought. If you answered with at least two or three (times per week/day) for the first two questions, then perhaps your inner good girl is responding more often than she should. If your answers for the following questions sounded something like, "often," "a lot," or "more than I'd like," then maybe it's time to start working your confidence muscle.

It's hard to break old patterns, so be patient with yourself! Just remind the good girl she deserves to feel strong. The human brain gets used to functioning in certain ways. If keeping quiet is what you've been accustomed to in group discussion, then the brain will dictate silence without you even thinking about it.

In order to build confidence, try doing the following for two weeks and see how you feel. It's helpful to expect that changes will be uncomfortable at first as you rewire your brain's response system. The good news is that over time you will strengthen your confidence, thereby empowering yourself and your sense of safety.

Here are some ways to work the confidence muscle:

———————— # ————————

1. When you disagree with someone, tell them so, and why.

2. Try saying "pardon me" instead of "I'm sorry." Nine times out of ten, we use "sorry" for very mundane and simple blunders like bumping into someone in the hallway. "Pardon me" will do just fine in those moments.

3. Engage in discussion with someone who thinks differently than you. This is a hard one, but I

guarantee you will be working a very important component of your confidence muscle. It doesn't have to be perfect. Just give it a shot!

----------------------------- # -----------------------------

Cultivating the Masculine Teddy Bear

All of the safety rules apply to both boys and girls. Boys, too, have to exercise caution in public spaces and listen to their intuition when a social situation feels uncomfortable. Boys, like girls, can experience assault with a perpetrator who may be a friend or family member, and need to feel that they can talk about it with someone safe.

However, there's a social factor that boys and young men face much more frequently than girls and young women: the absence of *healthy* touch. While an inappropriate touch can be emotionally scarring, a healthy touch can be affirming, validating, and necessary for good self-esteem. Yet boys and men are deprived of healthy touch more than they have ever been. With factors like homophobia and the stereotype around what it means to be tough or "cool," accessing healthy touch often means going against the social grain, and the results have been catastrophic.

Mark Greene, senior editor for *The Good Men Project*, explores the lack of gentle touch for men in his article "Why Men Need Platonic Touch." He writes:

We are not typically taught that we can touch and be touched as a platonic expression of joyful human contact. Accordingly, the very inappropriate over-sexualized touch our society fears runs rampant, reinforcing our culture's self-fulfilling prophecy against men and touch. Meanwhile, this inability to comfortably connect via touch has left men emotionally isolated, contributing to rampant rates of alcoholism, depression, and abuse.

Men need supportive, gentle touch as much as women do, but asking for it or giving it often falls outside the box of what is considered manly. For young men entering adulthood now, there's a lot of mixed messages to decipher around what is socially acceptable in the way of touch.

Masculine energy is one of the most beautiful forces on earth. At its best expression, it gives those near to it a sense of assurance, protection, and comfort. However, in our culture, unless one is a poet or musician, most men are not encouraged to express themselves emotionally. Imagine you are the guy hanging out with your male friends on a sunny summer day. Maybe you've just shot hoops. Maybe you're chilling out at the local park or swimming hole. Whatever you're doing, you're having a good time, and these friends have been in your life for a while, so you all know each other well. Can you imagine saying to your friend, Zach, "I just want you to know how much I value our friendship and love you as a person," and then giving Zach a big hug? If that's hard to picture, you're not alone. If that is how you normally act with your friends, bravo! You're living against the grain.

Ironically, this behavior is very common for girls. To say I love you and to touch and hug each other is a common facet to female friendship. Why can't the same be true for boys? The same feelings exist in friendships between males, as well as the need for love and affection. But often, boys are taught that touch can only exist in a male/female relationship and usually centers around sex. When you add pornography to the discussion, the problem gets even more complex.

The average young person has access to technology almost every waking hour, which means large doses of provocative images are available whenever one chooses to see them. #MeToo taught us that at the highest level of authority, sexual domination has been socially acceptable in this country and in much of the world. While it is never okay to cross someone else's boundaries, context matters. When the football players demand to know what the quarterback did with his girlfriend last weekend and why he hasn't had sex with her yet, or a couple of guy friends get intoxicated at a party and urge another to "have some fun" with the girl who drank too much, it's important to remember these behaviors take place in a culture that continues to devalue the safety of girls and women.

As of April 2019, according to KeyLogger Review, there are currently over twenty-four million pornography sites available online, prompting more than sixty-eight million daily searches. In 2010, a study analyzing the level of violence occurring in these videos found, "Of the 304 scenes analyzed, 88.2% contained physical aggression, principally spanking, gagging, and slapping, while 48.7% of scenes contained verbal aggression, primarily name-calling. Perpetrators of aggression were usually male, whereas targets of aggression were overwhelmingly female. Targets most often showed pleasure or responded neutrally to the aggression."

Since social media is the way we communicate, young adults are feeling more comfortable pushing the envelope of sexual self-expression. "Dick pics," exposed breasts, and flashing genitalia are flying across iPhone screens, but what's the underlying goal of this bravado? *Connection.* If we are conditioned to respond to other people in a certain way, we're not always conscious of how that impacts our behavior. As Mark Greene points out, if sex is the conditioned way we physically connect, then sex is going to get a lot of unnecessary and not-always-healthy attention from *both* sexes. Young men are given a bad rep for being hyper-sexual, but in many ways, they are only acting out the behaviors they observe in the media and that they see women engaging with as well.

Here are some questions to ask yourself regarding healthy touch:

———————— # ————————

1. When was the last time I gave a full bear hug to one of my guy friends?
2. Do I feel like I know how to give and receive healthy touch with others (men and women)?
3. How many times a week do I find myself looking at something on social media that my higher mind knows is demeaning to women?
4. Am I willing to be more safety-minded with what I expose myself to in the media?
5. Am I willing to stick up for women in a situation where there is risk?

———————— # ————————

If, as a young man, you can't remember the last time you really hugged one of your guy friends, give it a shot! It may surprise both of you that a hug feels comforting and connecting and is an appropriate way to express affection for each other.

If your answer to question three is at least a "two," then you have an opportunity to approach social media differently. This may mean that you are the odd man out with your guy friends, but it will increase the likelihood of healthy relationships with women.

If your answers to questions four and five were a solid "yes," well done! The very best aspect of your masculinity is able to show up when you become a champion. Champion behavior includes having respectful exchanges with women and being the guy who shows up as a protective force when the need arises. You may find your reputation among your female friends affords you a lot of positive attention when they see your inner champion emerge.

Safety in the LGBTQ Community

Since discrimination increases risk, safety protocol is especially important for people who identify as LGBTQ and gender-fluid. In 2015, The National Center for Transgender Equality found that almost half the participants in its sexual assault survey had been victims at some point in their lives.

Kristen Houser, chief public affairs officer at the National Sexual Violence Resource Center reports that "[b]ias and discrimination end up equaling secrecy and alienation, and when you don't have support systems... that often creates risk factors that people who inflict harm on others are seeking out. A queer teen who is shunned by his/her family and community is a more likely target for a sexual predator. A transgender person struggling to find employment is more likely to be homeless, which increases the risk of sexual victimization."

Discrimination requires that you strengthen safety protocol, whether you identify as male, female, or gender fluid. There are myths that sexual assault doesn't happen in same-sex relationships, but assault occurs when the abuser is seeking power and control, something just as likely to occur in same-sex relationships. Another myth involves the perception that gay men are effeminate and therefore not violent or that women are not violent and therefore not likely to be abusive. These are not true. People are people, and violent tendencies affect all sexes and all sexual orientations.

My friend Richard Downey (who identifies as "he") has been an advocate for the LGBTQ and gender-fluid community of Boston for more than thirty years. During that time, he worked at Aids Action and the Pine Street Inn while teaching dance classes at Harvard University. He talked to me about living as a gay man in Boston and how homophobia and transphobia affect safety:

> While a portion of our society may be more open-minded, homophobia is as alive and well now as it has ever been. I've had my nose broken by people who are homophobic. I've been spit at and called 'faggot' because being gay is thought of only as a sex act among homophobes.
>
> People like to tell you when you're young that 'it gets better' [living with homophobia], but it doesn't. *You* have to get better—better at making your internal reality healthy, better at making wise choices in relationships, better at knowing where you are and how to keep yourself safe. You can't expect that anything external is going to make being gay easy.
>
> A lot of people in the LGBTQ and gender-fluid community live with low self-esteem. We can be hyper-aware of what's happening around us all the time. We can be more inhibited.

Chemical disinhibitors like alcohol help people manage this hyper-awareness. But the false security they provide increases risk. There are often more sex drugs used in the gay community because they offset the self-loathing instilled by society. That's why it's so important to have a safety plan when going out for an evening, and enlist your friends to all keep an eye on each other. These safety plans are true for everyone, regardless of sexual orientation or identity.

The minute you feel uncomfortable in a social situation, get out of there. Never meet a date at their car. Always meet in a part of town where you are familiar with your surroundings. Always have money to take a taxi or an uber home. Keep your phone charged and have an exit plan when you go to a new place. If you go to a gay bar with a friend, know that you may not leave with that friend, so always have a plan for how to get home safely.

Because of the negative stigmas people in the LGBTQ community face, it can be harder to seek help when needed. There can be fewer resources and lack of support from family and friends, but local and national hotlines are there for support twenty-four hours a day. If you or someone you know has been assaulted or fears assault, don't hesitate to call. You have legal rights that the American Bar Association has made easy to access. Check out this detailed cheat sheet put out by the ABA—it can help you navigate a potentially abusive relationship and know what community supports are in place to keep you safe:

How do I know if I am in an abusive relationship? If my partner is:

- Threatening to "out" or outing the partner's sexual orientation and/or gender identity to their family, employer, or community
- Threatening to tell or telling others the partner's HIV/AIDS status
- Reinforcing fears that no one will help because she or he is lesbian, gay, bisexual, and/or transgender
- Telling the partner that abusive behavior is a normal part of lesbian, gay, bisexual, and/or transgender relationships

For other examples of abuse in LGBT relationships, see the LGBT Power and Control Wheel developed by the New York Gay and Lesbian Anti-Violence Project at www.avp.org, and click on "Issues."

What legal options do I have if I am afraid of my partner?

As an LGBT person who may be a victim of domestic violence, **you have legal rights,** regardless of whether you are married and/or in a recognized domestic partnership with your partner. Access to legal assistance will depend on the laws in your state.

A person can request protection from an abuser under both civil and criminal law. In almost all states, an LGBT victim can request a Civil Protection Order, an order available to victims of domestic violence that requires your partner to stay away from you. In most states, victims of stalking, repeated violence, or harassment can request a protection order which prevents the person from harming or contacting them.

What is a Civil Protection Order?

A Civil Protection Order is a civil court order requested by a victim (petitioner) and signed by a judge. A Civil Protection Order can, for example:

- Order the abuser to stop threatening, abusing, or harassing you
- Order the abuser to stay a certain distance from you (also known as a "stay-away order")
- Order the abuser not to come to your home (sometimes even if you share the home)
- Order the abuser to stop contacting you
- Say who your children will live with temporarily

For a summary of state laws on orders of protection for sexual assault survivors, as well as other options available to LGBT victims of domestic violence who are denied civil orders of protection, please visit **www.abanet.org/domviol** or **www.avp.org**.

Whether a transgender person can get a Civil Protection Order under a state's definition of relationship may depend on whether that person identifies or is legally categorized as the same sex as their partner. For example, a transgender woman who is legally female should have the same rights as a non-transgender woman to file against her abusive male partner.

What if I am afraid to get help because I believe that I will be harassed by the police for being LGBT?

Some victims may be hesitant to call the police or seek other assistance because they are afraid that they or their partner will be mistreated because of their sexual orientation and/or gender identity.

Legally, neither the courts nor the police can discriminate against victims and abusers because of their sexual orientation or preference.

Even with increasing efforts to eradicate homophobia and transphobia in police and court systems, many LGBT survivors still reasonably fear mistreatment by police and court systems. If you want to get help and do not want to contact the police or courts first, contact your local anti-violence program. These are groups that work specifically with LGBT survivors of domestic violence, sexual violence, and hate violence, and who can help you navigate the legal system.

To find your local program, contact the National Coalition of Anti-Violence Programs at www.avp.org or at the 24-hour hotline: 212-714-1141.

For help that is targeted to LGBT victims of violence, call the National Coalition of Anti-Violence Programs at **212-714-1141** for 24-hour assistance or visit http://www.avp.org/

Talking about safety *before* a risky situation presents itself makes it easier to broach the subject when and if you need to.

Here is a questionnaire that could apply to any young adult. Reflecting on your answers will let you know what areas may need additional safety-mindedness as an LGBTQ or gender-fluid person:

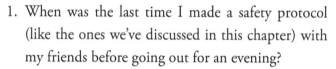

1. When was the last time I made a safety protocol (like the ones we've discussed in this chapter) with my friends before going out for an evening?
2. Have I ever met a date at their car?
3. Do I have confidence that I can talk to my friends or my family if I feel I'm at risk in my relationship?
4. Do I know someone in my circle who has been assaulted?
5. Do I feel confident that I would call an anti-violence hotline or seek legal support if I was ever assaulted?

———————————— # ————————————

Look over your answers. Is there room for increased safety with your friends and/or yourself? If someone you know has been assaulted, can you offer them feedback and assistance in finding the help they need? If you feel at-risk and are unsure about whether you can talk to friends and family, think about who you could talk to, such as a counselor at your college, an open-minded teacher, or a trained advocate at a local call center. Most college campuses have LGBT centers, and/or a similar organization located in a nearby town. On a broader scale, the National Center for Lesbian Rights and the Transgender Law Center provide advocacy to victims of discrimination. Whatever source feels right to you, determining the kinds of support that you have in your life is worthwhile, whether or not there's a current need for it.

CHAPTER

5

Developing Herd Consciousness

Safety-mindedness does not have to equal *boring*. As a young person, lifestyle choices are often made that involve spontaneous adventure, including the kind that push safety boundaries, but there's a way to have fun and still avoid risk. This chapter is devoted to developing the kind of strategic thinking that helps young people support young people. I call it herd consciousness.

Animals of prey never let down their guard entirely while grazing in open fields. Although young adults don't have to fear losing a limb to a fast-running cheetah, they can cultivate the same kind of group power to avoid danger. Most people don't head out under the stars on a Saturday night thinking about how to stay clear of sexual assault, nor do they necessarily need to, but there are safety tools to use as a group that render such thoughts moot. If your herd consciousness is functioning at capacity, there's no reason why you can't whoop it up with the best of 'em on that starry night out.

So how do we "work the herd?" The answer is straightforward, simple, and much like the antelope do:

remember that your friends are also your power group, and that means everyone is responsible to keep alert.

Let's say Linda and Sally have offered to take Nicole out to a house party since she just broke up with her boyfriend and is feeling down. If Nicole ends up having too much to drink and is flirting like a diva with an unknown guy, it's up to Linda and Sally to make sure that Nicole leaves the venue with her friends at her side, even if she protests. This is the kind of agreement that can be made ahead of time with your power-group. If Nicole is certain she wants to spend time with this stranger on another date, great. She can meet him for coffee when she's sober, after her two good friends help her to arrive home safe that night.

Another scenario: let's say that two just-friends, Ben and Jonas, head out to a local gay bar to mingle and let loose for an evening. They're having a grand time when suddenly Ben notices that Jonas is acting strangely. He's having trouble staying seated at the barstool and doesn't make sense when he talks. Ben can assume something was slipped into Jonas' drink and step in to get Jonas out of that situation and to a medical facility before something unfortunate happens.

Both of these situations are in some ways no-brainers, but when you're out on the town having a lot of fun, it's easy to lose track of each other unless your herd instinct is intact. If Sally and Linda got caught up with the party and failed to notice that Nicole slipped out the back door with her flirty stranger, they'd end up with a case of lifelong regret if Nicole got hurt.

Most often, the assault stories I've heard in my practice involve a small group of friends (at least two people) going out for an evening, during which, at some point, one of them got left behind with a guy they were flirting with. The rest of the group, who may have been drinking or involved in their own fun, thought this friend wanted to be left alone, but this was not so.

My client Marie (whose name has been changed to protect her privacy) wanted me to share her story. At the age of fifteen, Marie was out with a girlfriend. This girlfriend was eighteen and dating a twenty-two-year-old. The twenty-two-year-old boyfriend asked if he could bring a friend along for the evening, to which the young women said yes. All four commenced to drinking at the boyfriend's apartment. Marie's girlfriend was off in another room fooling around with her boyfriend, and Marie was left alone with his friend. Marie suddenly knew something wasn't right because of how she felt.

Marie recalls, "These two men 'ordered' alcohol and had it dropped off at the apartment, which at fifteen, I didn't know was strange. It arrived in a brown paper bag and we let them make each of us a drink. I only had half of one drink before I started to feel funny. I remember saying things that didn't make sense and laughing a lot. I didn't feel like I had control over my body. I felt like a rag doll. I couldn't even stand up. I blacked out after that and don't remember anything else, other than I woke up the next the morning in my friend's bed."

Marie was a virgin when she was drugged and raped three doors down from her friend who left her alone with a stranger. The simplest of actions could have prevented an outcome that affected Marie for the rest of her life. Since that time, she reports struggling with anxiety and poor relationship choices. Claiming her personal authority has been difficult because of the assault at age fifteen. Marie is now finding ways to empower herself and not give in to the fear that used to get the better of her. She is learning how to go from being a "victim" to being a "survivor."

It never seems like a big deal at the time, but leaving someone alone in a situation like this (even if it seems like your friend wants you to) can have devastating consequences. Herd consciousness means looking out for each other. When practiced, it can literally save your friends' lives.

Here are some ways you can "work the herd":

———————————— # ————————————

- Talk to each other before going out. Assess how everyone is doing with the basics—food, water, and energy level. If one of you is dehydrated or neglected to eat properly that day and your plans do not involve an immediate meal, take care of this easy fix before going out.

- Establish your protocol before arriving at an event. For example, agree to check in with each other through text or in person if you get separated, and make sure your phones are fully charged beforehand.

- At a club, always know where the exits are and have a plan to circle back with each other at a given location and time.

- Have a secret signal. If someone outside your group is getting too friendly or one of you is feeling uncomfortable and there isn't the opportunity to talk, have a signal that you can give each other (i.e., an ear tug) that functions as an alert—"Get me outta here!"

- Support each other when a report is needed either by calling the police, alerting a bar owner, or bringing in other people that are safe. When it looks like calling the police might be necessary, don't hesitate. Make the call. You could be saving a life.

- Keep your phone on you, even if you're with your power group. Remember that users running iOS 11 or higher on iPhone devices can access an "Emergency SOS" option by pressing the lock button five times.

#

Sexual Safety and Substance Use

Even if you were the uber-conservative girl or boy in high school who never inhaled a puff of a cigarette or a joint and only took sips of wine at home in the safe harbor of family, it's more than likely that at some point in your college or early career, you'll find yourself in a social situation where trying something new feels *normal*. Most people who experiment with substances do so out of curiosity, to experience an altered state of consciousness, especially when so many others are doing the same. So, in looking at life after eighteen and the likelihood of substance use, we must keep it real. Most young adults have or will experiment with at least alcohol, so it's best to operate from *what is* in discussing safety.

Did you know that, according to Alcohol.org, half of sexual assaults involve alcohol use on the part of the victim and sixty-three percent of offenders were under the influence at the time? Since substance use is a known part of life after high school, what can your power group do to decrease risk? Here's a full description of two of the biggies:

---- # ----

1. If drinking, have your beverage in your hands at all times. Going to a frat party? Bring your own beverage container, with a lid. You don't have to worry about being the odd man or woman out. There have been enough horror stories like Marie's,

of someone slipping a roofie (a.k.a. "date rape drug") or other substance into an unsuspecting victim's drink. A roofie (officially named Rohypnol) is a tranquilizer about ten times more potent than Valium. The effects start twenty to thirty minutes after taking the drug, peak within two hours, and can persist for eight or even twelve hours, during which the person may be aware of what is happening but is powerless to defend themselves. Afterward, memory is impaired, and the victim cannot recall any of what happened. Drugs used to incapacitate people can be odorless, colorless, and tasteless, so you can't rely on your senses to tell you that someone slipped something into your drink. The consequences aren't worth it. Bring the lid.

2. Watch out for the members of your group when someone has had too much to drink. Safety becomes an issue when people are drunk enough to be disoriented, so, *pace yourselves*. Drinking water throughout the evening helps ensure that you stay aware of your surroundings.

———————————— # ————————————

Even with safety measures in place, rest assured (if you haven't already), you will at some point witness someone you know going over the edge with a substance, most likely alcohol. This is where your power group takes on a much wider definition. Let's start with….

What Do You Do with the Drunk Girl?

We've all seen her. She's the girl at the party who doesn't seem to know when to stop drinking. She might become so drunk because she hasn't had enough to eat that day or a guy interested in her is making her drinks *really* strong. She may be going through an emotional challenge and for many people, regardless of age, drinking is a form of escape. No matter how she arrived at inebriation, the drunk girl (DG) is likely to engage in some unsettling behaviors. She might get on stage with the band or DJ and start singing along and dancing wildly. She might say something outlandish and obnoxious. She might rip her shirt off or make out with random strangers. She might get so out of control that a stone-cold sober person would equate her behavior to a public nosebleed—we just want it to go *away*.

Here's the thing about the DG, though: she isn't displaying behavior that's any different from what a drunk *guy* might do, but for some reason, people tend to have less patience with drunk girls. This fact is wrapped up in our understanding of female decorum and the projection we've put on girls since time immemorial: good girls are demure and quiet; bad girls are loud and messy. Our DG, nine times out of ten, will fall in the latter camp. The difference between the drunk guy and the drunk girl is that the guy who drinks too much and engages in all these messy behaviors is likely to be joined by a small band of his posse who will egg him on, laugh at his behaviors, or even join in, creating a noisy throng of testosterone-driven and alcohol-fueled man-boys who might later declare what a great party it was (for them).

The drunk girl will be left to her own devices.

As hard as it is to intervene, this is where sisterhood shows its true teeth. The DG should never, *ever*, be left to her own devices. She is the one most likely to end up passed out in someone's bedroom, and the next morning she will have no memory of what happened or why her pants aren't on. This should never be a *thing* and is not "normal" behavior.

So, sisters, as hard as it is to handle the DG, handle her we must, regardless of whether she is a friend or a stranger, because a drunk guy will likely be strong enough to protect himself in a dangerous situation, but a drunk girl will not.

Here is a list of some practical responses that may make it easier for you to intervene to assist the DG:

———————— # ————————

1. Start with a friendly check-in: "Hey, how are you doing? You seem pretty intoxicated; can I get you some water so you don't have a screaming headache tomorrow?"

2. Keep a watchful eye. Are you noticing that people are coming on to the DG or that she seems unable to walk properly? This is a great time to ask her to step away to talk with you. "Hey, I want to show you something," you can say, or "I think pizza just arrived," or "Lisa brought her pet monkey; wanna see him?" Say anything to get the DG out of the situation. As uncomfortable as it may be to spend time with her when she is that out of it, you may very well be preventing an assault that could affect the rest of her life and yours.

3. Grab a group of sisters and lead her out of the house, dorm, or club, even if she is resistant. Offer kindness, whether or not you feel it, saying, "We care about your safety and are not gonna leave you alone, whether you like it or not."

---- # ----

What Do You Do with the Blacked-Out Boy?

If I could go back and re-write history, I'd erase every story I've ever heard in my therapy practice that involved one or two people getting "black-out drunk." Of course, the potential for this behavior crosses all gender categories, but for the sake of brotherhood, I'd like to discuss how it affects young men specifically and what safety-conscious guys can do.

Perhaps you've heard of Brock Turner. Turner was a freshman at Stanford University and a star swimmer on his way to the 2016 Olympics. Turner assaulted twenty-two-year-old Chanel Miller outside a frat party after both had been drinking. Miller was unconscious when Turner left her by a dumpster after being chased from the scene by two young cyclists. In his court statement, Turner blamed alcohol as the reason for the assault. In her testimony, Miller admonishes Turner, saying, "If you are confused about whether a girl can consent, see if she can speak an entire sentence. You couldn't even do that. … I was too drunk to consent before I hit the ground."

The judge on the Turner case received nation-wide public outcry when Turner was released from county jail just three months after he was found guilty. However, what the court failed to do was, in part, made up for by the courageous activism of Chanel Miller (whose victim impact statement aired on 60 Minutes), and the public rejection of her assailant. USA swimming effectively banned Turner from ever competing for the US again. He is not allowed to step foot on Stanford campus, and his name will remain on the sex offender's list for the rest of his life.

In contrast to this kind of unfortunate story, men who use the power of their masculinity to *protect* women from harm possess very attractive character traits. Showing up as a safe presence sends a powerful message to your posse: threatening girls isn't cool.

So, men, help your brother and yourself stay on the champion's side of masculinity. Your relationships with both men and women will stay healthy when you support safety protocol. No one wants jail time or to scar another person, potentially for life. When it comes to a situation where a person is physically or sexually vulnerable, show up as their protector, whether or not you even know or like them. Mark my words, it will come back to you a hundred-fold.

The following are some guy-to-guy statements to use when behaviors are looking risky:

---------------- # ----------------

1. "I see how wasted you are, and I'm staying by you tonight so you don't do something stupid."
2. "I'm gonna take your car keys, but if I see you grabbing at Jerica the way you do when you're drunk, I'll call you out on it on the spot."
3. "You're better than this. I can tell you're making her uncomfortable. Let's get outta here and regroup for a second. I promise if you change how you're acting, I'll leave you alone."

---------------- # ----------------

When something becomes "normal" we stop talking about how to fix it, even if we know it to be wrong. Regardless of gender or sexual orientation, when someone gets black-out drunk before "fooling around" with someone else who has not soberly consented, they not only put themselves at risk of incarceration but also put the victim at risk of long-term psychological damage. Did you know that the U.S. government spends more money on sexual trauma treatment than it does on any other violent crime? From the victim's perspective, when the bender is over and the morning has come, so has the potential for enduring PTSD symptoms. Using safety-minded thinking and positive group energy helps to keep such situations at bay.

Here are some self-to-self questions that apply to all gender categories and will help you best use your power group:

———————— # ————————

1. Do my friends and I have a check-in with each other about substance use before going out for an evening?
2. Do we all tend to keep an eye on each other when we are in a party atmosphere?
3. Have I ever seen a close friend get black-out drunk? How did that make me feel?
4. Do I believe my power group uses safety-minded thinking when it comes to drugs and alcohol? If not, am I comfortable with that?

5. Is my power group consistent about always having a designated driver, which means having a sober member of the group?

———————————— # ————————————

Check your responses. If the answers to the first two questions were "no," ask yourself, "Can I talk to my power group about using better safety methods?"

If question three made you realize you don't like it when friends get black-out drunk, you deserve to let someone in your power group know. You might be starting a conversation that helps everyone since everyone deserves to be comfortable socializing together. If the answers to questions four and/or five are "no," take a moment to ask, "Can I have a conversation with my friends about using substances wisely?"

When it comes to sexual safety, everyone needs a protocol with drugs and alcohol. Even if you are determined to remain abstinent, you will still need a clear set of boundaries for yourself in case you are the odd person out. You have a right to make your own choices and stand by them no matter what, even if it means making sure a few trusted people have your back when the answer for you is "no."

To all readers, I say in the name of safety: if you want to experiment, please never ingest a substance for the first time without a group of safe and trusted people around you. Have a power group of at least one or two friends with you so if something goes wrong, there are others who can, hopefully, handle the situation in a safe and trusted way.

How to Work Your Community

College is a limited and somewhat uniform space. So is home. You and your power group will be having more and more experiences in the communities within which your college and home exist. Sometimes, a risky situation can be avoided by knowing how community organizations work and how to use them in a mindful way. Here are some basic examples:

------------------------------ # ------------------------------

- Know the public transit system and avoid stops that are in questionable areas or have minimal visibility.
- Know where the local police station is located.
- Keep a fund so that you always have money for an Uber or taxi if public transport seems questionable.
- Know your "blue-light zones." On college campuses, there are well-known blue-light phone boxes to use to call for help in the case of an emergency. You should also have the campus police number saved in your phone contacts.
- Off-campus, there are almost always well-lit public spaces to go to in case of danger. All-night markets,

gas stations, restaurants, or even clubs are a way to be visible to the public in a moment of risk.

- If you are someone who likes to be in-the-know, you can keep the app on your phone that tracks potential sex offenders in your area, known as the Offender Locator Lite. Just be aware of your tendency for anxiety if knowing equates with increased fear. The point is to be aware, not afraid. The rest of your safety protocol will go a long way in protecting you whether or not you use the locator app.

———————— # ————————

No organization designed to respond, such as the local police or hospital, could possibly take care of everything you or your friends might need in handling a dangerous situation. This is where family and trusted people in authority can aid you. It is also where your power group is most effective—by letting its members get the support they need through open communication with each other, even with a statement as simple as "I need help."

CHAPTER

6

Know Thyself

Turning eighteen is nothing short of *awesome*. At no other time in life are we more poised for new experiences, information, and self-development, all while being fully independent for the first time. With adulthood, we get to function as both pilot and co-pilot by taking the self we know into the big, wide world and trying it on for size. I hope this chapter will help to hone your flight skills and give you ways to maneuver the occasional cloud cover that is an inevitable part of the ride.

Let's start by returning to the most important three words in the sexual assault description: *unwanted sexual touch*. The unfortunate truth is that some people reading this have already been touched by someone in a way that makes the word "unwanted" seem trivial. While I hope this hasn't happened to you, I also hope that if it has, you try to talk about it with someone you trust. Sexual assault can leave the kind of scars that aren't visible but cause long-lasting pain, especially when kept secret. The mind is not able to heal itself when the burden of secrecy weighs heavy, which is why I have included a chapter on response later in this book.

When we are compromised, our defense system is compromised. Being safety-minded means being aware of the times you might be tired, improperly fed, dehydrated, or sick. In those moments, you're less perceptive to things around you, which means you'll be less apt to notice if something goes wrong. On a day when you feel fatigued, you may avoid running extra errands after work or school. So if you're at a party or social event that night, let your group know you're not functioning at full capacity. Tell your friends you're not feeling well or are run-down. They can agree to check in on you or respond if it seems like you might be in an uncomfortable situation. In short, your friends have your back when you're not feeling well, and you have theirs when the situation is reversed.

There are deeper aspects to knowing oneself beyond sickness or fatigue, and these play an important role in safety protocol. For example, if friends say you're naïve, innocent, even gullible, it may sound like a mild insult but could also be a valuable safety tool.

Knowing yourself means taking an honest inventory of how sheltered you've been and whether you're ready to take risks you haven't prepared for yet. In other words, if you want to backpack alone through South America, and you've never left the hometown where you grew up, that's awesome!, but you may want to take a self-defense course first.

Avoiding the Freeze

Have you ever been in a situation where you didn't know what to do or say and your body seemed to just freeze? This could have happened to you while watching a fist-fight at school. Or perhaps a teacher got pushy in class one day and insisted you come up with an answer but asked it in a demanding way, like, "Hurry up, we are all waiting for you." Even if you know the answer, you might find yourself momentarily speechless.

In psychology class, you may have learned that this deer-in-the-headlights reaction is a function of the hypothalamus where the defensive part of the brain is located. When the hypothalamus anticipates a threat, numerous stress hormones are released, causing a surge of anxiety. Anxiety can lead to the desire to fight (i.e. yelling back at the pushy teacher) or take flight (i.e. freezing without response). It may sound like the "flight" part of the limbic brain would mean running away from the situation. Although this could happen, a lot of times flight is experienced instead as a bodily shutdown. When there is enough fear, the normal coping mechanisms we use to handle tough situations become hard to access, and we freeze.

Knowing our response patterns provides greater safety in a risky situation. If someone is more of a "fight" type, they can look at how to support that pattern in a healthy way. Self-defense classes, kick-boxing, and martial arts all serve to better utilize the fight response system when it comes to a high-risk situation. For people who are prone to freezing, it's equally important to speak up when caught in a freeze moment. Even saying the word "No!" or "Stop!" loudly can break the freeze long enough to allow for other reactions like calling for help.

Here are some self-to-self questions regarding fight or flight:

———————— # ————————

1. Am I more of a flight person or a fight person?
2. Have I ever been in an uncomfortable position because of my fight or flight reaction?
3. What can I do to work with my defense patterns so I can be safe even if I feel scared?
4. If I am prone to freezing, how can I practice speaking up when something triggers that reaction?
5. If I am more of a fight person, how can I channel that to support myself and others in feeling safe?

———————— # ————————

Look at your answers. If you are generally more fight than flight, you may want to cultivate that in a healthy way by taking a martial arts or kickboxing class, and if you are more flight than fight, you can practice breaking the brain's freeze response. I guarantee there are other people in your power group who react the same when it comes to flight, which means you can help each other work the confidence muscle we discussed earlier. To break the freeze response and work your confidence, practice speaking up in class, telling someone when you disagree with their opinion, or asking for space when someone crosses your personal boundaries. I promise that the more you do this, the easier it gets!

One way to understand our brain's defensive reactions and the way our bodies communicate danger is by describing "low tone" and "high tone" response. Low tone reactions are experienced as calm, while high tone reactions are experienced as fear, agitation, or anxiety. At any moment of any given day, our defensive reactions are giving us signals that register as either low tone ("I'm so relaxed sitting with my friends, enjoying a fruit smoothie") or high tone ("I'm on alert because there's a really loud woman at the table next to us yelling at her children"). Hopefully, in our everyday lives, we are more often registering calm, but it's helpful to notice when low tone becomes high tone and all the variations in between.

In my sexual assault prevention classes, I ask students to do a roleplay where they stand at a distance from someone they know and trust. Then I ask one to walk toward the other slowly. The one who is standing still is asked to put his/her hand up when the other feels like they are getting too close. When the activity partners know one another, hands usually go up within three feet of each other. Suddenly, low tone has gone to high tone. The reason this happens is that our bodies have an energy field I call the "safety bubble." Even someone we know and trust who crosses this boundary can cause a high tone reaction. Imagine, then, if someone we didn't know got too close. We might register a high tone response at five to seven feet.

We'll continue to discuss high tone and low tone throughout this book. For now, try noticing what your body is signaling when it comes to your personal safety bubble. Although we all have these energy fields, some people have a harder time deciphering theirs. They may have been exposed to a lot of yelling in their family and won't notice the loud woman sitting at the neighboring table yelling at her children. To them, yelling is normal. However, if hearing a lot of yelling in childhood also meant getting hit, their high tone reaction might get extreme quickly, bordering on an anxiety attack. These folks have probably spent a lot of time learning how to manage their high tone reactions.

Whether your high tone has been muted or is over-active due to the experiences you've had in early life, building tone awareness can strengthen your ability to know whether or not a situation is safe. Try tuning in when you're out in public or with a group of friends. You'll notice that certain places raise your tone level, and there are certain people you won't want to cross your personal safety bubble. You can also roleplay with your friends and notice how your responses differ. As with everything else we've discussed so far, when it comes to tone awareness, practice makes all the difference in the world!

Tool Kits (a.k.a. Knowledge Is Power, and Self-Knowledge Is Empowerment!)

Long ago, in a far-away land called the nineteen nineties, I was a young twenty-something living in Boston. I had lots of friends who were local, since Boston was essentially my hometown. Because my apartment was near to Fenway Park and Lansdowne street, I also had access to some of the best nightclubs the city had to offer. Each weekend, my friends and I could usually be found working off our nine to five jobs by dancing, especially since we knew "the clubs" like we knew our own living rooms.

It never ceased to amaze me, back then, that guys felt free to grab me by the waist and pull me toward them while I happily let loose on the dance floor. Dancing seemed to mean a free pass to grope, grab and generally *invade* the space I occupied. It took a short while for me to realize I needed more common sense when out clubbing. I began to make sure that I never strayed far from my group and let my body language indicate I had no interest in anyone other than the friends I was with, and the amazing musical geniuses of the era, such as Nirvana, Luscious Jackson and Prince.

We don't usually think about tools when we think about sexual assault prevention, but some of our most important tools aren't carried in a purse or backpack. They exist inside us and can make a big difference in a moment of risk. Some of these tools are part of our personality and we don't have to work for them at all. Others don't exactly come naturally. The good news is that humans are adaptable creatures, and our brains have the capacity to learn new information and acquire new skills almost magically; it just takes a little focus and determination.

Here are some of the most important internal tools we carry:

--- # ---

- Common sense
- Gut instinct
- Affect manipulation
- People perception
- Communication

--- # ---

Most of these tools are well-known, and by the time we are teenagers, we probably have a sense of just how equipped we are with any one of them. Still, some are not as simple to understand. Take *affect manipulation* for example. The best way to describe this is to tell a story my friend Caroline shared with me.

Caroline was in her early twenties when she spent two weeks in Spain traveling around, looking at the beautiful coastal towns of the south, and eating large quantities of fresh fish that had been caught from the sea and grilled that afternoon. It was a lovely adventure, and for the most part, she felt safe. There were a couple of times, though, when she had to *manipulate* her affect while walking through a public space. Like many countries, it is considered normal in Spain to cat-call women, stare, and/or make crude jokes. At least, it was when Caroline was there.

One day, the behavior went on a little longer than she was comfortable with, and a group of men began following her down the street. She started to get scared, but before anything else happened, Caroline turned around and yelled as loud as she could in Spanish, "Hey, jerks! If you take one more step to follow me, I will call the police!" The gang snickered at her, but they did not go any farther. Of course, there are many other tools one could use in this situation, but for Caroline, she knew she had to get tough to let that group know they couldn't walk around threatening her by their presence, and her tactic worked.

Other times while traveling, young people are encouraged to manipulate their affect even when not in a threatening situation. If you're walking down the street with your chin up and your shoulders back, assuming an air of "don't even think about messing with me," people will notice. Again, it isn't designed to guarantee safety, but it's a great start. Usually, people find that even if they have to "fake it 'til they make it" with copping a tough attitude, the more they do it, the tougher they feel. In short, attitude matters, and we all have the capability to manipulate our outer appearance so that we *look* much less vulnerable than we may at times *feel*.

So, how about *people perception*?

Have you ever gone to a party and met someone who rubbed you the wrong way? Maybe you couldn't quite put your finger on it, but something about that person gave you the creeps. Your people perception skills were working in your favor to create a "cringe" response. While it's true that our people perception may not always be accurate, it's worth listening to that inner voice that says, "I'm not comfortable with this person." Sometimes, these reactions can occur with people that are supposed to be "safe," like a family doctor, a youth group leader, a priest, or a coach. If you feel a high level of discomfort with any of these individuals, chances are your people perception skills are warning you something may not be right. Then, it becomes necessary to communicate how you feel. A parent or teacher may be able to intervene to create a different outcome in the situation. Bottom line: there is never a time when being uncomfortable means you have to suck it up and continue to place yourself in a circumstance that doesn't feel safe to you.

The best way to be safety-minded is to use multiple tools simultaneously. Often, tools like *people perception* are combined with tools like *gut instinct*, and we don't even know we're doing it.

Youth and *common sense* don't usually get equated together, but there are ways the new generation has more common sense than their elders (as many in my generation can attest to). Still, there is a value to lived experience. For example, I had to learn as a young person, that I had every right to let loose when out dancing, and that didn't mean, "come touch me." Once I figured that out, I was able to have more fun. My friend group grew closer and I discovered how to trust my instincts about strangers I met on the dance floor. I learned that sometimes, happy people like to be around other happy people, and those are the moments when safe strangers can become great new friends. When I had the opposite instinct, however, I learned not to waste any time sending mixed signals.

Here are some *common sense* practices that allow you to exercise the power of your free will and still enjoy yourself:

――――――――――― # ―――――――――――

1. Never allow yourself to be alone with someone who makes you uncomfortable or is threatening you.
2. Stay in proximity to your friends if going to a party or club.
3. If someone you don't know well is texting you provocative images, block them and consider reporting it.
4. Don't let someone you just met buy you a drink. If you enjoy talking with them and the gesture feels

genuine, *you* can order and have the bartender serve you, then *they* can pay the tab.

Gut instinct (or intuition) is a tool that is so important, it's worth checking in with several times a day. Ask yourself, how is my gut responding right now to the situation I'm in? Since our cognitive "muscles" work much like our physical muscles, the more we use them, the stronger they get. This is especially true with gut instinct. Practice checking in with yourself on what your intuition is saying. Use your gut instinct to improve your *people perception*, and let that inform your *affect manipulation*. Most important: *communicate* with the people in your life exactly what your gut instinct is trying to say. You will improve your flight skills so much that being safety-minded will become second nature!

Here are some helpful questions to get you thinking about your inner safety tools:

1. How often have I been in a situation where someone rubbed me the wrong way, but I didn't say anything about it to anyone?
2. Would I describe myself as having good common sense? If not, what are some specific areas of development that I can work on?

3. Have I ever tried to look tough even when I felt scared? Did making myself look tough actually help me feel tougher?

4. How often do I tell my friends when I have a gut instinct reaction to something?

5. Do I trust my gut instinct or intuition? If not, what do I need to do to work that response mechanism so I can use it if I'm in an unsafe situation?

———————— # ————————

Your answers provide helpful information about managing your internal safety tools. If your answer to question one was "often" or "many times," don't sweat it! You have everything you need inside you to begin doing things differently; it's just a matter of practice. If your answer to question two was "no," same thing! Becoming an observer of people and places will help you build your common sense. If you don't think it's very strong yet, that just means you haven't had a chance to develop it. Be patient and start to play out certain scenarios with your power group or with yourself. What would each of you do if you were on a date and your date started giving you the creeps? What would you all do if someone was invading your space at a frat party? What happens when you try looking tough in a new situation or when you're walking down an unfamiliar street? And most importantly, how connected do you feel to your intuition? This is the most important safety tool you can use when meeting new people.

Safety and Dating Practice

Most people take step-by-step advances toward adulthood. By age five, you might attend your first sleepover party. By age ten, you know that life with your parents has an endpoint, and by the time you graduate high school, you know that figuring out the right kind of person to date sometimes means dating the wrong kind of person first. Perception is a learned trait, and sometimes people make wrong choices before determining what the right ones are. In this chapter, you will hone the perception skills needed to shorten the arrival of those right choices. Rebellious urges are part of the "adulting" process, which means there will be times when deliberately making wrong choices feels fun and even necessary, but sexual risk-taking isn't one of them. Far too many people have had to learn the hard way that being rebellious with one's sexuality can have devastating consequences.

Social Media

At the most fundamental level, dating entails good ol' trial and error and the hope that things will work out in your favor when meeting someone new. Meanwhile, on a palm-size screen, your dating life is being managed, observed, accounted for, and responded to 24/7/365.

Growing up with social media has incredible benefits, but there are challenges too. Someone on their phone or tablet might be less aware of what's happening off-screen and miss an important social cue, which is why most young adults have trained themselves to do both actions simultaneously: pause to check in with current surroundings, and still maintain use of their phone.

Cyberbullying is a more difficult challenge. Did you know that seventy-six percent of women under the age of thirty have reported experiencing online cyberbullying, unwanted contact, trolling, sexual harassment, and threats of rape? We often hear stories in the news that involve sexual assaults being videotaped by the perpetrator and posted all over social media.

A 2013 article in *Rolling Stone* entitled "Sexting, Shame and Suicide" told the especially tragic story of fifteen-year-old Audrie Pott. Audrie was sexually assaulted by a group of her classmates at a house party. Afterward, she had to endure the secondary trauma of seeing photos of the assault as they circulated around her high school in Saratoga, California. A week later, Audrie committed suicide, the only way she could see getting out of her personal nightmare.

The photos that were posted by her classmates the week before Audrie's death make *Lord of the Flies* look like kindergarten summer camp. One depicted a knife wound that had been photo-shopped to her neck with the words "you should just kill yourself" posted beneath. How anyone could possess enough hate to post something like that is a mystery. What we do know is that social media has made for some dangerous outcomes that require everyone—male, female, gender fluid, gay, or straight—to be consistently safety-minded with their online presence. How?

———————— # ————————

- Keep your privacy settings active on your phone.
- Make sure your Snapchat location is set to ghost mode or only includes your closest friends.
- Never allow strangers to have access to your contact information.
- Always use your intuition when meeting new people and give yourself enough time with them to confirm that your intuition is right.

———————— # ————————

Another facet of social media becoming increasingly popular is the posting of naked pictures. Sharing nude or semi-nude pictures online can cause damages that are rarely anticipated in advance. By the time you enter college, you have likely heard at least one story about someone's nude photos being shared more broadly than intended. This type of exposure crosses all gender categories. Young women are just as likely to engage in nude picture taking as young men. What people forget is that sharing naked pictures is against the law, can lead to jail time and a permanent record, along with significantly harming your chances of future employment, since most employers check social media and online sources before hiring.

Carrie Goldberg, New York attorney and director of the Cyber Civil Rights Institute, advises victims of cyber harassment to record the evidence. If you're aware that photos of you are being broadcast online, take screenshots of the posts and relevant internet search results for your name. Record URLs and messages. Save this information on your computer, but also print out a copy to take to the police.

"With the exception of hacking cases, ninety-nine percent of the time victims know exactly who is responsible, and it's very provable with IP [addresses], login, and other cyber forensic information," Goldberg said in an interview with CNN in 2017.

Think more than twice about letting someone film or take pictures of your naked body. These are not for posterity. A long-term committed relationship with privacy settings in place is one thing, but even then, you can never guarantee the relationship won't one day go sour, leaving the potential for those intimate pictures to be shared with someone you would never want to see them. Remember: once it's online, you can't take it back again.

Mindful Dating

It doesn't take an investigative reporter to observe that the average young person is *busy*. Job commitments, extra-curriculars, and social and familial obligations are daily realities, to say nothing of college requirements, which are now more competitive than ever. Since early childhood, many people have learned that success takes drive, focus, and a lot of preparation. If you're not figuring your way into the game, then you're at risk of sitting it out, which is why when you talk to most young adults these days, they will likely share that they have a plan. This plan could be college, travel, or time off. It could be waitressing for a year while decidedly *not* figuring anything out. These are nonetheless *plans*, and a lot people in the new generation are serious about carrying them out.

It's harder to have a plan when it comes to dating because you could land in a whole heap of trouble if your plan turns out to be wrong. By now while reading this book, you've learned about fight or flight, gender roles, how to identify low tone/high tone responses, and how to use your power group to avoid risk. In this final section, we get to see how all of that plays out in regards to dating. It's worth having a few tools that ensure you're on the right path and, when it comes to safety, that you're the one calling the shots as far as sexual readiness.

I wish I could send this chapter to all the women I've worked with who told me their sexual lines were crossed because in the moment they "didn't know" what was right or wrong or how to stop. The scenario usually begins with two people fooling around, engaging in behaviors like kissing and light petting, behaviors that produce arousal. With erectile function, there's no mystery as to whether a guy is turned on or not, whereas with women the signals are subtle. Regardless of how turned on she might be, at this point of the fooling-around session, the difficulty comes in determining two things:

---------------- # ----------------

1. Now that the guy is turned on, is he going to get off (meaning orgasm)?
2. Whose job is it to make that happen?

---------------- # ----------------

This is the point at which a woman might be told that since she "started it," she now has to "finish the job." Suddenly, the mutually gratifying experience becomes one-sided. At that point, the pressure of the performance duties placed on the woman can induce a stress response, making it difficult to access her true feelings and needs. Instead, the immediacy of the demands creates a deer-in-the-headlights reaction.

So, women, if a guy tells you he has "blue balls" and it's your job to take care of him, do you believe him? With all due respect, *No!* If at that point, you'd rather be home painting your toenails, remind him that he has a hand and he knows how to use it. In short, masturbation is his answer, not pressuring you to take care of something he can do for himself.

The same rules apply to young men. Plenty of manipulative ladies are out there who use sex as a weapon for control and self-satisfaction. Be careful of the woman who comes on strong when you are uninterested. There could be an ulterior motive (like she wants to make her ex jealous or she is struggling with low self-esteem) that has less to do with your needs and everything to do with hers. If the motivation behind pushing you to have sex feels sketchy, remember that following through with her wishes could come back to bite you.

Sexual energy is among the strongest forces on earth and, at its best expression, beautiful beyond measure. Sex brings us closer to our romantic partners in ways that no human language can, but since the body is primarily a pleasure-seeking organism, the brain can trail a little farther behind in the get-to-know-you phase of dating. If the warning signs are starting to show, know that there are behaviors that can help you stay safe when and if it looks like your boundaries might be crossed.

For example, look out for the guy or girl who tells you what they think you should wear or how often you should see your friends. While this may not lead to sexual assault, it's an indicator of an unhealthy behavior that could very well play out in your sex life. There are plenty of other people to date who will respect your choices without trying to manipulate you. When it comes to the guy or girl who "loves" by control, there are words for this kind of thing, and love has nothing to do with it.

In American culture, sex is lucrative, reliable, stimulating, and available in some form nearly all the time, but that doesn't mean we know how to safeguard the relationships that contain the sex experience. There's almost nothing more exquisite than two people in love for the first time, and the best aspects of that beautiful new relationship are probably not about *sex*. However, sex gets a lot of the attention. Exploring the ways your relationship grows in other areas can be wonderful to observe. Meanwhile, although our culture will encourage you to focus on sex, it's up to you to decide how much you're willing to listen.

While every young adult is probably aware of the need for boundaries in a new relationship, the particulars will look different for everyone. One young man may promise himself that he will only date someone his friends approve of. One young woman might declare she has to be with someone who gives her a lot of attention, and vice versa. Someone else may plainly establish what their sexual boundaries are with a new lover. Regardless of the many expressions of self-protection, self-interest, and personal choice, there are a few fundamental pieces of straight talk that every young person should hear:

———————— # ————————

1. Be aware of your level of naïveté.
2. Be aware of your experiences with older people.
3. Be aware of the requests made by a new potential partner early in the relationship.
4. Most importantly: be aware of what your defense system and high/low tone intuition are telling you about someone new or about someone you already know.

———————— # ————————

Most assaults take place with a known offender, which is part of the reason so few are reported; there's a relationship at stake, and too often, victims feel they must suck it up and stay silent in order to protect the "friend" who has hurt them.

My client Jamie (whose name has been changed) was in college when she was sexually assaulted by this type of friend. They had known each other awhile, and he had expressed romantic interest in Jamie, to which she respectfully said she didn't feel the same way. This conversation happened a few more times, and each time, Jamie clearly stated her boundary—they were just friends.

Jamie got sick and was laid up in her girlfriend's home when this admirer came over, went to the room where she was resting, and asked Jaime to have sex with him. In talking to me about her experience that night, Jamie said, "In college, there are so many 'firsts' as you're exploring new things. You're meeting a lot of new people as you recreate your tribe away from home. This guy was a friend and a classmate, and I saw him every day. He was nice and likable, and I never thought he would have pushed it that far. I was so feverish and out of it. I had medicine in my system and could hardly move, but he was relentless. I told him no, but he kept pushing. Finally, I said 'fine,' but it wasn't what I wanted. I thought I didn't have a way out of it unless I gave in. After that night, I don't recall seeing him again."

For Jamie, it wasn't until her twelve-year-old daughter received an inappropriate text from a classmate that she realized how much of her own story had yet to be healed. Jamie panicked out of concern for her daughter but was then able to connect with her own assault history in a more conscious way. As is clear, Jamie was compromised with fever and therefore *incapacitated*. She was not able to provide consent, which classifies her experience as sexual assault.

Red flags are different for everyone. A lot of times, women may not know the difference between feeling nervous and feeling creeped out, so they blame themselves when they're uncomfortable. All of our safety tools come into play when managing friendships and dating new people. With a new romantic partner, our people perception, gut instinct, common sense and high tone/low tone awareness are crucial in making the kinds of choices that serve us beyond the present moment. But what about the distraction of desire?

There are at least a dozen things that can detract us from listening to our inner voice at any given moment, and desire is only one of them. Whether external or internal, humans have greater capacity than any other living creature to be caught by the allure of distraction. We can find ourselves changing how we normally behave in order to align with a person we want to impress. The consequences of this may vary depending on the person or type of distraction.

By way of mild example, any time I made a wrong choice about a piece of clothing, there was always a small voice inside that said I might not wear the article that looked so pretty in the store once I brought it home—but desire won out over whether the item was a fit for me. Consequently, it used to be that every year I had a bag of Goodwill clothes in my closet made up of the purchases I thought were just right at the time but then I never wore. I had to learn how to exercise caution in buying the things that were right for me versus the ones I desired to be right.

On a much larger scale, dating choices function the same way. Sometimes what we lose with great heartache because it wasn't a fit, eventually comes back in the form of a healthier, happier relationship—starting with ourselves.

Here are some fundamental tips to use in your dating life. Notice that all of the tools in your safety kit can apply when meeting someone new:

Common Sense

- Remember to let your roommate or a friend know when you are going out on a date with someone you've just met. Keep your phone charged and your location settings on.
- If you're out with someone new, have your power group agree on a signal (like an emoji) that indicates trouble, should you need to alert each other immediately.
- Always meet a new date at a public place you are familiar with.

Gut Instinct

- Regularly check in with your low tone and high tone. Start to build awareness of the types of people and situations that create high tone reactions.
- Trust your gut! If someone is creating a high tone response, tell them to back off.
- Practice listening to your intuition and track how often it is taking care of you by giving you accurate signals.

Affect Manipulation

- If you feel uncomfortable out on a date with someone who is giving you lots of high tone response, *manipulate your affect* by not letting on that you're creeped out. Give yourself time and means to exit the scene. For example, casually remark that you promised your roommate you'd check in to see how her sick mom is doing, excuse yourself to go make a phone call, and leave.

- Group dates are always an option. If out for the first time with someone you don't know and are unsure of, lightly suggest that your friend and their partner come along to create more fun as a group. Your date never has to know this suggestion came because you're unsure of them.

People Perception

- Know yourself and the type of people you're drawn to. If you haven't had the greatest track record with those you've dated, you can work on your people perception skills.

- Discuss with your friends the types of choices you are making in your dating life. Exploring people perception skills as a group can help each of you understand the reasons for these choices and how to make better ones if you need to.

Communication

- Always remember to work with your power group, even if it is composed of only one other person. For example, if you and your roommate have agreed to let each other have use of the dorm room in order to invite a date over, continue to check in and communicate as roommates. Make sure the agreement hasn't become one-sided and is still working for *both of you*.

- Practice communicating your true feelings if someone you're with makes an obnoxious remark. Notice your internal signals and let them know it made you uncomfortable or ask what they meant by the statement. Speaking up will accomplish three things: 1) the building of your assertive self-protection response (or righteous anger); 2) improving the awareness that your perceptions are correct; and 3) obtaining information as to whether this person will respect your boundaries or not.

Safety Challenge

- Check out the above categories and identify two that you know are challenging for you. Rest assured, you're not alone! We all have areas of strength and weakness.

- If you can determine that there's room for improvement in any two categories, try writing a journal entry today about how you perceive each of them. For example, it could be memories you have of, say, *not* listening to your gut instinct or times when you forgot to tune in to your gut response and things went poorly.

- Try working that tool as much as possible for one week. Make a point of checking in with your gut reactions and see where they lead.
- At the end of the week, write another entry. Notice anything that is different after you've had the chance to practice the tool for a sustained period of time. I bet you will observe *big* changes.

CHAPTER

8 How to Respond to Assault

The Importance of Reporting

When it comes to sexual assault, secrecy can work like cancer cells that grow over time, impacting the whole psychological system. Each day, thousands of assaults go unreported because of shame, embarrassment, or fear of repercussions, and countless victims suffer needlessly by keeping the truth locked inside themselves. I hope you never experience this type of violence, but if you or someone you love does, there are supports in place you can turn to. In this chapter, we'll talk about response tactics and how to know what choices are right for you and/or those close to you.

My friend Lily, who we talked about earlier, reported her assault at the church soup kitchen immediately after it took place. Lily was surrounded by teachers, parents, and classmates who supported her in following through with the necessary legal steps. She was able to see that there were procedures in place to ensure the perpetrator be punished, and that hopefully, other potential victims would be kept safe because that report was made.

Since then, Lily hasn't shown any sign that the assault scarred her or was damaging to her mental health. She finished the school year successfully and was able to have an enjoyable spring season, complete with college tours, academic awards, and nailing a great summer job. Nothing about Lily's assault was a secret to the people she was closest to, so nothing had to be worked through on her own. It's not easy for a young person to think about entering a police station to fill out a report against someone they know, or to tell their advisor a fellow student sexually harassed them, but speaking to the people who can do something about it provides a greater sense of safety. In short, talking about hard things keeps worse things from happening.

In responding to potential or actual threats, it's important to know the organizations that are there to help you. The police force and the local court are designed to work together in these cases. When an assault has taken place, the best immediate action is to seek medical attention, if needed, and then to make a report with the local police.

The following is from the Sexual Assault Support Services of Midcoast Maine, a local sexual assault response organization: "First and foremost: seek medical attention for possible injuries, pregnancy, STDs, or for the collection of evidence as soon as possible. If you can, take a trusted friend with you so that you are supported in working with the medical staff you may have just met. When you go to make a police report, it's important to not wash, urinate, douche, brush your teeth, eat, drink, smoke, or change clothes because it can impact evidence."

This is all frightening to think about and difficult to write, but you'll want to give the investigating officers as much information as possible in order to file charges. Of course, you have a right to make a police report at any point, but faster reporting time can impact an investigation.

Aside from reporting, try to talk to a trusted parent, teacher, guidance counselor, or family member. Whatever adult you choose as your "point person," it's helpful to know you're with a team of people (even if it's only one or two others) assisting you.

Keep in mind there are circumstances where making a report is necessary, and some have nothing to do with *responding* to assault. People are encouraged to make police reports when they feel threatened, harassed, or targeted by someone they view as unsafe. Verbal threats or harassment are enough to call in a report, and harassment includes someone following you down the street or texting you after you've asked them to stop.

Bottom line: if you feel unsafe, *tell* someone.

National Hotlines for Filing a Confidential Report

According to RAINN (Rape, Abuse and Incest National Network), only 19.5% of assaults take place with a complete stranger. When an assault involves a known offender, like a classmate, a coach, or a TA, it can be doubly challenging to report the crime. No matter what, sexual assault is never the fault of the victim, and there are agencies in place to make it easier to file a report. Sometimes, it just means finding the right friend to help you take the steps that are hard to take on your own. For those who have difficulty finding a point person because they are more solitary, or haven't made friends in their new environment yet, the local and national organizations designed to respond have trained personnel who are fully equipped to provide the compassionate support such circumstances require.

Aside from dialing 911 in an emergency and/or contacting the local police, RAINN is a national organization committed to responding to assault in a way that protects the victim. The following information is from their website, rainn.org. Look it over and consider whether you have any questions; if so, RAINN has trained advocates on staff who can answer them for you.

How Does Reporting with RAINN Work?

When you call 800.656.HOPE (4673), you'll be routed to a local RAINN affiliate organization based on the first six digits of your phone number. Cellphone callers have the option to enter the ZIP code of their current location to more accurately locate the nearest sexual assault service provider.

Calling the National Sexual Assault Hotline gives you access to a range of free services including:

———————— # ————————

- Confidential support from a trained staff member
- Support finding a local health facility that is trained to care for survivors of sexual assault and offers services like sexual assault forensic exams
- Someone to help you talk through what happened
- Local resources that can assist with your next steps toward healing and recovery
- Referrals for long-term support in your area
- Information about the laws in your community
- Basic information about medical concerns

———————— # ————————

The One Time There Are *No* Rules

If you are ever in a situation where you are forced to protect yourself from harm, please remember, anything goes. Countless assaults have been thwarted because the potential victim was able to fight the offender off or escape to safety. If cornered in a room by someone who is dangerous, don't wait until you've been hurt. It may seem like a no-brainer to assume that you would fight back, but the freeze response can be a very real obstacle to self-defense. If you're someone who is prone to freezing, it's worth considering how you would counteract this reaction.

What are some self-defense moves to call on? A swift kick to the groin, a hard wrist or fist to the chin, or an elbow to the gut are acts of self-defense that could save your life. If you're in a location where other people are nearby, screaming for help or shouting "RAPE!" will be more likely to keep you safe than staying silent. If on a street and able to get away from the assailant, *run*. If you're in a public setting, the chances are slim that you'll be chased.

It may sound extreme, but self-defense laws are there for a reason, and finding your inner mojo to get vicious will go farther than you think. This is why humans have been known to lift cars off the ground when someone they love is trapped underneath. In the same way, there are many people who have avoided rape by fighting their way to safety. When in danger, call on your superhuman strength to do all you can to protect the person you love—*you*.

In addition, self-defense classes, model mugging courses, kickboxing, or martial arts classes are like merit badges on your safety vest. Any one of them will increase your sense of confidence in knowing how to respond to risk and how best to apply your strength. There are no rules when it comes to safety, and you have a right to use whatever means necessary. Talking with friends and even practicing a sequence of moves (such as what I described above) will familiarize you with the basics of self-defense applicable to any face-to-face scenario with someone trying to threaten you.

The more that students, parents, and teachers support each other in taking the issue of sexual safety seriously, the more "normal" safety measures become. College safety forums and constructive family conversations play a huge role in helping young people feel comfortable talking about assault prevention, as do supportive friendships. Still, no matter how careful we are or how much we've cultivated safety-mindedness, we can't guarantee our friends' safety all of the time, so it's important to know what to look for if someone you care about has been hurt.

I Think My Friend Was Assaulted, but They Won't Talk about It

If someone you are close to has been assaulted, it may initially be too difficult for them to talk about. You might observe changes in their behavior that lead you to think something happened, although they aren't opening up about much of anything.

As we discussed earlier, the autonomic nervous system of the brain can function differently following assault. For example, if the offender was driving a royal blue sports car at the time of the incident, the trauma brain might register fear each time a royal blue car drives by. Brain scans indicate that the executive function of the frontal lobe essentially goes "offline" in those moments, creating a freeze reaction or an overwhelm of anxiety. Trauma-related anxiety, when it is severe, functions like the terrifying school bully who waits for his chance to attack, no matter how many alternative hallways are taken to avoid him.

While these types of scars look different for everyone, there are common features and red flags to know about in case you suspect one of your friends may be in trouble.

Your friend might:

———————————— # ————————————

1. Suddenly lose or gain a lot of weight.
2. Date partners who abuse them through violence, addiction, or both.
3. Start to struggle with addiction themselves.
4. Unexpectedly "freeze," or disassociate, or have difficulty making decisions.
5. Have either highly loose or highly rigid boundaries.
6. Show signs of depression, suicidality, or self-harming behaviors.

———————————— # ————————————

After the assault in the field when I was eight-years-old, I don't remember having any trauma effects in the days and weeks following, but I can remember every detail of that afternoon, so I know in some ways, it never left me. I still see the way the sun fell on the tall yellow grass of the overgrown section in our backyard, and the manicured space of green next to it where my father mowed and where the boys held me down. I can see the clubhouse that was behind me and the wall of trees bordering our property on three sides, blocking all other houses from view.

Most of all, I remember how loud I screamed, knowing that we lived at the end of a dead-end street where no one was likely to hear me. Even at age eight, though I don't remember ever being told, I knew such things could happen to girls, and I knew that boys were almost always stronger. In the years since, I've had to address my trauma brain reactions and learn how to calm myself when irrational fear gets the better of me. Over time, I learned to trust the wisdom of my higher mind. My trauma brain can create some wildly distorted perceptions, but my wise mind is always accurate, always stronger, even if in the moment, it doesn't feel that way.

Effective Treatments for Trauma Recovery

Western culture's manufacturing of sex and beauty as power masks the reality of sexual violence, while those who suffer from the effects of trauma can feel like they're standing on the side of a fast-moving highway, watching as others move forward in life while they are standing in quicksand.

Healing from these emotional and mental wounds requires love, patience, and self-compassion. One part of the brain has to convince another part how not to live in fear. Trauma expert and author of *The Body Keeps the Score*, Dr. Bessel van der Kolk, describes the need for therapists to assist their clients in connecting with their emotions and the high-level processing part of the brain, even when the body and the limbic system are colluding in a fight or flight reaction. He states, "Only the executive functioning part of the brain can access the animal brain. …And only when you know your interiority can you have a life."

This is why treatments such as cognitive behavioral therapy (CBT) are popular, especially when combined with bodywork. With CBT, the client uses their brain's executive functioning to implement techniques that comfort the frightened surges of the animal brain. Healthy replacement behaviors can support new responses to trauma triggers. Slowly, and with a lot of patience, the individual learns to retrain their reaction patterns so as to live a calmer life.

Cognitive Processing Therapy (CPT) achieves the same goal, only through a different channel. Jaime Lowe is a writer for the *New York Times* and the author of *Mental*, a memoir about living with bipolar disorder. On August 26, 2019, *This American Life* aired a program titled "Ten Sessions," in which Lowe recorded her cognitive processing therapy with a trauma clinician. The program is mind-blowing. In her treatment, Lowe was able to see the "stuck points" where her thinking had become distorted as a result of the trauma she endured at thirteen when she was assaulted in an alley near her home. According to Lowe, the goal of CPT is for the client to "change the story you've been telling yourself about what happened." Since fifty percent of women who experience sexual assault develop PTSD symptoms, working with the "trauma brain" that tends to write its own script is a crucial part of the healing process.

Still, all of the brain work in the world can't help an assault survivor learn how to inhabit their body, which is why most trauma therapists recommend bodywork as a part of treatment.

At around the time I first shared my story of the assault in the field, I also discovered the practice of yoga and, no coincidence, was immediately hooked. Fast forward a couple decades, I'm now certified to teach Kundalini yoga and have probably logged a few thousand hours on the mat. For me, no other form of bodywork comes close to offering what yoga does. Even now, if traveling away from home, my family knows we aren't going to get far without the yoga mat.

Recently, in an online trauma training with Bessel van der Kolk, I learned yoga and mindfulness practice are some of the most effective trauma treatments we have. Through calming breath and slow movement, the practitioner learns to inhabit their body in new ways. Over time, the mind/body connection supports a sense of internal stability rather than fear. Other healing forms such as Phenomenal Touch massage, Chi-Gong and Reiki have their own ways of creating inner calm and connection. The important thing is to find the type of bodywork that feels like a fit for you and make it a steady part of the weekly routine.

Here's a quiz to get you thinking about thought patterns and the ways you relate to your animal brain:

———————————— # ————————————

1. When I get anxious, how do I use my thoughts to calm myself down?
2. Do I think the methods I use to center myself work most of the time?
3. Have I ever tried using my executive brain to assist my animal brain in lowering my anxiety?
4. Does healthy bodywork help me center myself? Do I have enough physical outlets in my life now to support my executive brain functioning?
5. What are my thoughts on yoga and/or meditation? Do I believe I could benefit from these practices?

———————————— # ————————————

By answering these questions, you're on your way to developing the kind of personal wisdom that makes for greater safety, but also greater confidence. Knowing how to maximize your inner calm is crucial in today's high-pressure society. Cultivating the skills needed to manage the pressure creates an independence that is more assured, self-aware, and empowered.

Managing Obstacles

The Invisibility Cloak

My client Rebecca had been in therapy for more than a year before she shared her assault history with me. By then, she was in her mid-thirties and had spent most of her life with what she described as a small inner sense of "invisibility." Raised in a family where women were expected to look pretty and, for the most part, keep quiet, Rebecca was victim to the good girl phenomenon long before she was victim to assault. According to RAINN, ninety percent of rape victims are female, which makes sexual assault one of the biggest gender equality issues of our time. Millions of women like Rebecca live with invisibility cloaks that perhaps no one in their lives even knows exist.

The good news for Rebecca is that she was committed to her own healing. After sharing her history in a therapeutic format, she started to experience shifts with the internal shame voice that always said, "Keep quiet and don't draw attention to yourself, that way you'll be safe." Instead, Rebecca started speaking out more. She created an innovative program within her professional organization, set new boundaries in her romantic relationship, and became an advocate for greater safety in her community.

Rebecca states, "I feel like I was walked over forever, and was taught how to be a doormat. Now, I'm committed to my healing and growth. I'm breaking the cycle of shame and self-doubt for myself and my son. The urge to put my invisibility cloak back on still surfaces from time to time, but I now recognize it does more damage than good. Instead, I'm becoming empowered by my voice. I was naive to think that not speaking up about my assaults would make them go away or make me look weak. It's just the opposite: by speaking up about my assaults, I have become stronger in every way."

Rebecca began to have a whole new life once the invisibility cloak came off. Getting past the obstacle of shame has allowed many survivors to claim a more empowered personal journey, for it is self-trust and commitment that heal the human soul.

A Man's World

Sexism is that subtle beast that can inhabit the most liberal of minds when the right situation presents itself. Even an avid feminist can encounter another woman in Starbucks wearing high heels, a face full of make-up, and a tight skirt, and might observe to herself that the other is "sleazy." Because of the power of sex and advertising, women receive unfair judgment for their appearance, even from open-minded women. In order to be aware of patriarchy, a not-so-subtle under-layer affecting all of society, we must have a vigilant inner-scope to avoid the possibility of *victim-blaming*.

As we know, victims can also blame themselves, creating internal "stuck points" that affect everyday life. In between the lines of those self-statements, we find internalized sexism rear its head. Here are some examples:

---- # ----

- "If I wasn't dressed inappropriately, I wouldn't have been assaulted."
- "If I hadn't been drinking at all, I would have been safe."
- "I shouldn't have been nice. They got the wrong impression."

---- # ----

Victim blaming is the reason women and members of the LGBTQ community are more likely to experience assault. For many offenders, it's easier to be violent against someone they believe is a "slut," "whore," or "faggot." These terms make the victim something less than human and, therefore, fair game. All manner of misdirected anger is channeled through the brutality of sexual violence, especially for these two groups.

Harvey Weinstein is a great example. Lust wasn't the primary driving force behind Weinstein's assaults—power and misogyny were. At present, more than fifty women have come forward with allegations that Weinstein forced himself on them, in sometimes "pathetic and revolting" ways, using power to his advantage as he threatened the women's careers, even their lives. According to British actress Lysette Anthony, who Weinstein reportedly attacked in her London home in the late 1980s, the assault left her "disgusted and embarrassed."

Lucia Evans was an aspiring actress in 2004 when Weinstein summoned her to his office for what she thought was a casting meeting. She reports she was then forced to perform oral sex on Weinstein. Evans later told *The New Yorker*, "The type of control he exerted, it was very real."

Emmy-nominated actress Annabella Sciorra alleged that Weinstein forced himself into her apartment in New York in 1992 and raped her. She told *The New Yorker* how ashamed she felt afterward, even though she tried to fight him off. "Still I was like, why did I open that door?" said Sciorra, blaming herself.

Clearly, even women in the spotlight can experience victim-blaming and shame, which is why #MeToo was a necessary force in bringing the truth to light. My guess is that behind Weinstein's bravado and intimidation lives a very insecure and fragile ego. Now, the movie mogul has a lost empire, millions of dollars in settlement costs, twenty-three years in prison, and a name synonymous with "sexual villain."

Weinstein's fall can give us new hope. A 2018 *New York Times* headline said it best: "#MeToo Brought Down 201 Powerful Men. Nearly Half of Their Replacements Are Women."

At least eleven states, including California and Vermont, passed new protections addressing workplace harassment. Prevention education is now available in grade schools. The changes we've seen came about because people were willing to get uncomfortable, which means we can anticipate more discomfort as we continue to move forward.

The Challenges to Reporting

When it comes to speaking out, a primary obstacle for college students is *reporting*. Variables that don't affect the population at large become major stumbling blocks for the co-ed whose entire life centers around the square footage of their college campus. When your friends (and possible enemies) are the people you live with, eat with, socialize with, and attend classes with, upsetting the petri dish becomes a very big deal.

The Department of Justice (DOJ) conducted a study in 2007 to determine why sexual assaults are not reported more often. They found that college students gave six primary reasons:

———————— # ————————

1. Victims did not have proof that the incident occurred.
2. Victims were afraid of retaliation by the perpetrator.
3. Victims were scared of hostile treatment by the authorities.
4. Victims were uncertain the authorities would consider the incident serious enough.
5. Victims wanted to prevent family and others from learning about their assault.
6. Victims didn't know how to report the incident.

———————— # ————————

Overall, the DOJ concluded that "fear and confusion" were the biggest obstacles to reporting and that many college students don't understand the legal definition of assault. The study prompted colleges and universities to create more robust prevention protocols, which many schools have implemented. But again, we have farther to go. This is where taking the initiative goes a long way in keeping you safe. Discussing prevention protocol among friends ensures that you won't be the one who is too uncomfortable to be informed. Having read through this safety guide, you can feel emboldened. You now have more knowledge than most of the population when it comes to sexual safety.

10

Becoming a Movement Maker

Going Ashore

Let's imagine that you're back on the bow of your ship, making your way to the beautiful island we described at the beginning of the book. The wind fills your sails as you're carried closer to shore. In your binoculars, you can make out the coastline and see the beach where your magnificent conch shell rests. You've traveled far to get here and have taken time to know the island and its make-up. You've studied its topography and weather patterns, the rise and fall of the trees beyond the shore, and the details of the beach where you'll make land and find your conch shell amid the rocks.

You've learned about the obstacles that may get in the way as you retrieve your shell. The cultural forces we discussed in the last chapter are there to test you and make the journey more difficult, but you've done enough navigating and exploring to figure out your way around them. Even if at times you get lost or an obstacle seems like it looms too large to manage on your own, you have tools you can use to lessen the burden, ask for help, and find your way back to your path.

Now, your job is to continue the adventure. Explore your new island. Get acquainted with its inhabitants. Find the clearing in the trees where you'll make your camp, whether that's a temporary resting spot or a permanent dwelling. Locate the trails you prefer to take to get from place to place. Learn who your new tribe members will be and who will be part of your inner circle. These are all necessary aspects of your new journey of discovery. The only other thing required is that you carry your shell with you. It is unique in all the world—no other shell has existed, or ever will, that is quite like it. Now you know how to keep it safe.

You have a whole set of tools in your arsenal to call on. You've learned about the socio-cultural factors that influence our society. You know how to work with your friend group in ways that keep everyone safe. Most importantly, you know your personal weak spots and what the stronger parts of you can do when those weak spots affect your safety.

Even with all the safety methods in place, there will still be times when it seems as though you've lost your beautiful conch shell. Perhaps you're the woman whose inner good girl kept quiet when her boundaries were crossed. Or perhaps you are the man who has fallen so deeply in love, he can't see his partner is using him. These are the moments when it seems you've lost your way entirely, but not to worry. All you have to do is fetch the binoculars from the ship's bow and look at the scene from a distance. You can always find your shell when you make a point to try because your relationship with it is everlasting.

In the times you feel momentarily lost, look for what I call "mirrors." These are the people, places, and things in your life that help you return to *you*. Any time you need them, your mirrors are there to guide you back home. Of course, there are mirrors you haven't met yet as well. Being wise with your tools—like people perception and gut instinct—will go far in accessing the right mirrors at the right time.

To help you continue your journey in protecting your conch shell, here are some daily safety tips to use along the way:

---------------------------- # ----------------------------

- Practice your *communication* and *people perception* skills when in the company of others.
- Remember how your mind works in moments of stress and call on the wisdom of your executive brain to counteract the animal brain.
- Continue to cultivate the inner tools of *common sense* and *gut instinct* when out for an evening.
- Try speaking out when you feel threatened or intimidated by someone.

- Have discussions with friends who are equally invested in keeping their own shells safe.

––––––––––––––––––––– # –––––––––––––––––––––

Think about any positive change that has ever happened in the world. It came about because of everyday people, like you and me, who saw a problem and decided to fix it. Tarana Burke, the originator of the term "Me Too," has worked for over two decades empowering victims to become survivors. Now that she is more in the spotlight, Burke encourages people from all walks of life to join her in being a positive force for change. In an interview with The Guardian, Burke stated, "There is inherent strength in agency. And #MeToo, in a lot of ways, is about agency. It's not about giving up your agency, it's about claiming it."

All of the great activists and social change agents throughout history were movement makers on a large-scale, karmic course, and the effects of their efforts still impact us to this day. But movement makers exist in all forms. The everyday people variety may be less well-known and less visible, but are no less important.

When we talk about sexual safety, we integrate the tools. When we speak up for the person being threatened, especially if it's ourselves, we become a champion. These behaviors are difficult to carry out when caught in a moment of peer pressure but are necessary in becoming the kind of movement-maker that changes the world.

Here are some champion moves that will get easier the more you do them:

———————— # ————————

- Be the person at the party who stays near to the girl who got intoxicated and makes sure she gets home safely.
- Be the one in a group who calls out someone else making a sexist joke.
- Be the friend who accompanies another friend in going to the police station to file a report.
- Be the friend who uses tough love to confront the person they care about who's engaging in risky behavior.
- Be the woman who knows it's not her job to please a man sexually if she doesn't want to.

———————— # ————————

There is still one fundamental, irritating, and hard-to-solve problem that gets in the way of champion behavior more than anything else, and that is *caring too much about what other people think.*

Valuing others' opinions instead of being true to yourself will cause you to lose your conch shell every time, and this is where support is most needed. Friends can help friends recover and, if the situation warrants, connect with the family and community members that are best able to assist. By creating the space where young people feel the support they need to talk about their concerns, a proper plan can be made.

Being a Movement-Maker with Parents and Caring Adults

We live in a culture that doesn't yet have language for discussing sexual safety, and the legal system designed to protect us doesn't always work properly. Legal systems often involve miles of red tape, and even when we persevere, we may not achieve the desired outcome.

While you are wise to trust the local municipalities and organizations that are there to keep you safe, such as schools, churches, libraries, and the local police and court system, none of these are foolproof. Being a movement-maker means getting comfortable talking about uncomfortable topics, even with people you might not normally speak to about those issues, such as parents, teachers, and other adults who care about you.

Just remember that part of *your* personal protocol is to have boundaries, especially when working through a difficult time. Let your caring adults know that they're not allowed to repeatedly ask if you are okay, if you've slept or eaten enough, or have enough warm clothing. Adults are famous for hovering around the basic needs list when they think their younger ones are in trouble. I know; it's annoying. However, you now have all the tools to be the initiator of the conversation when *you* decide you're ready.

If talking to a parent or family member isn't possible, look for safe people in your college or home community. The organizational supports we talked about earlier are also available if it feels like the burden of secrecy weighs heavy.

Frank Warren can teach us a lot about the need to share secrets. In 2005, Warren started PostSecret, a blog site made up of anonymously received secrets. He wanted to see what would happen if he invited people to share their secrets via individually designed postcards. Between 2005 and 2007, Frank received 2,500 postcards. Now, hundreds of thousands of cards are stacked in his office with more coming every day. Proof that secrecy is indeed a heavy load to carry, and proof that thousands of families have stories they may never have shared with anyone.

Movement-makers can help a culture rooted in puritanism open up to the truth so that secrets don't have to be burdens. Talking about the reality of assault helps keep young people safe by letting them know that no secret is too horrible to share, and no offender is worth protecting at the expense of oneself. Parents and teachers are wise to engage in dialogue that is not patronizing or overly simplistic, for in many ways the members of the new generation are already movement-makers capable of great things.

Talking with Friends

I hope this book was able to provide conversational tools in response to the conversational awkwardness that now exists around sexual safety. Through reading each chapter, you've likely been doing your own personal inventory on how the information applies to you, and what the most important tools are for your life. I call that developing your wise mind. You now have options and protocol choices that are entirely up to you, and can be applied in any given moment.

However developed your wise mind thinking has become, it may still be difficult striking up a conversation with friends on the subject of sexual safety. If you are in a supportive group, you should feel able to say whatever you need, or try asking one of the following five questions as a way of breaking the ice (notice the possible responses for each):

———————— # ————————

1. Have you ever felt afraid that your sexual boundaries were in danger of getting crossed?
   - Now, if indeed someone has had their boundaries crossed, they may not want to go any farther than this. If they wanted to talk about it, a second question could be, "Are you open to talking about that?" after which the person could share their story. Otherwise, you are not asking them to share details, only whether or not they have had this type of experience.
2. Are you aware of how those experiences have affected you?

- Here, the question still does not imply a desire to hear what the experience was, only whether they are aware of how it affected them.

3. Do you think the response to the event (by you, your family, and friends) was helpful? If not, why?
   - Again, this is still not asking for more details.

4. Do you think that you've learned from that experience in a way that makes you feel safer than you did before?
   - If not, what's missing?

5. If you could give yourself additional knowledge regarding sexual safety, what would it be?

———————————— # ————————————

Any one of these questions will open the doors of conversation. Otherwise, when it comes to a friend you are worried about who may have endured trauma, asking a simple, "I'm here for you. Please tell me how I can help?" goes a long way. After all, friendships are the gardens of our soul, including the friendships we have with family members. Widening the doorway of conversation offers layer upon layer of healing for those who need to talk.

The New Generation

Everything is just beginning as you prepare for the next chapter in life. Whether that means college or travel, work or volunteering, whatever you undertake will shape you in ways that determine your destiny and the chapter choices you make after this one. Nothing should hold you back or burden you as you soar.

You're now equipped to better enjoy the healthy relationships you develop and prevent the kinds you don't want. You have, hopefully, a new understanding of yourself that you can bring to all the relationships in your life, whether with family, friends, or lovers.

All that I can add by way of closure is a blessing.

May you live loud and proud as you navigate the island of your making. No one knows how to do that better than you.

Acknowledgments

Be Strong, Be Wise began with the gathering of stories, some I read about and some I already knew, that all represented millions of other stories. The individuals who chose to share theirs here gave the book its spirit through difficult, yet heart-felt, honesty.

I'm thankful for the expert counsel from my new tribe of writers, Gro Flatebo, Susan Casey, Rita Saliba, Jean Peck, Barbara Walsh, Nancy Brown and Pat Hager, whose skilled love of the craft encouraged me to take the paths less comfortable, but necessary. Special acknowledgement to Susan Casey for giving the manuscript its final edit, and for supporting the project on every possible level, from the beginning. Ora North, developmental editor, helped to imbue the book's framework with deeper meaning. Managing editors, Bethany Davis and Emily Tuttle, refined its accessibility for the reader. Thank you to Angela Lauria and The Author Incubator's team, as well as to David Hancock and the Morgan James Publishing team for helping me bring *Be Strong, Be Wise* to print.

The book would never have started, let alone finish, without the support of those closest to me. My family were the patient, keepers of the faith who endured the obsessive constancy I bring to a writing project. To my daughter, Anikka, a heart full of thanks for your consistent encouragement. You inspire me daily with the unique strength and wisdom of the new generation. To Duane, my beloved, it was you who taught me to believe in the power of self-trust.

Finally, I'm grateful to the Source energy that inspires human connection and prompts us to tell the truth.

Thank You

By reading this book, you've decreased the likelihood that you could be among the many people harmed each year by sexual violence.

If you'd like to learn more about the safety steps, or know of others who could benefit, contact me for information on the *Be Strong, Be Wise* program. Following the book's principles, the program is designed for any group, including college students, counselors, sororities and fraternities, teaching faculty, or a circle of friends. By integrating the tools and refining the self-knowledge that empowers young people to be informed rather than afraid, the *Be Strong, Be Wise* program supports a safer, freer independence on every level.

The initial call is free, so don't hesitate to reach out! Here's how to find me:

Web address: http://www.bestrongbewise.com

Email: amy@bestrongbewise.com

Twitter @bestrongbewise

Personal web address: https://www.amycarpenter.net

About the Author

Amy Carpenter brings twenty-five years of experience to her new book, *Be Strong, Be Wise*, and the *Be Strong, Be Wise* safety education program. A psychotherapist, former youth worker, writer and life coach, Amy has written articles for PsychCentral, the Asana International Yoga Journal, and 3HO.org, where she's a contributing blogger. Amy is currently seeking representation for two previously-written books: *Glen Stone*, a middle-grade novel, and *Channel Crossing*, a parenting book. She lives in Rockport, Maine, with her husband and daughter. Find her at bestrongbewise.com or amycarpenter.net.

References

http://Alcohol.org

Alyssa Milano Looks Back at #MeToo Explosion. Associated Press Interview. October 3, 2018.

The American Bar Association. www.americanbar.org.

The American Civil Liberties Union. https://www.aclu.org.

Barbash, Eyssa. *Overcoming Sexual Assault: Symptoms and Recovery*. Psychology Today. April 18, 2017.

Bridges AJ, Wosnitzer R, Scharrer E, Sun C, Liberman R. *Aggression and sexual behavior in best-selling pornography videos: a content analysis update*. Violence Against Women. October 16, 2010.

Brockes, Emma. *#MeToo founder Tarana Burke: 'You have to use your privilege to serve other people.'* The Guardian. January 15, 2018.

Burleigh, Nina. *Sexting, Shame and Suicide: A shocking tale of sexual assault in the Digital Age*. Rolling Stone Magazine. September 17, 2017.

Carlsen, Audrey; Salam, Maya; Miller, Claire Cain; Lu, Denise; Ngu, Ash; Patel, Jugal K.; Wichter, Zach. *#MeToo Brought Down 201 Powerful Men. Nearly Half of Their Replacements Are Women*. The New York Times. October 23, 2018, updated October 29, 2018.

Chanel Miller reads her entire victim impact statement. 60 Minutes. September, 2019.

Dastagir, Alia E. *She was Sexually Assaulted within Months of Coming out. She isn't Alone.* USA Today. June 13, 2018.

Everfi. *6 Reasons Why College Students Don't Report Assault.* October 15, 2018. https://everfi.com/insights/blog/students-dont-report-sexual-assault/

Fox, Rebecca. *So What Do You Do, Frank Warren, Founder, PostSecret Project?*

In a weird way, the secrets give me strength. Media Bistro.

Hanna, Jason. *What you can do if someone posts an explicit image of you online.* CNN. March 12, 2017.

Harvey Weinstein scandal: Who has accused him of What? BBC News. January 10, 2019.

The Legal Dictionary. https://legal-dictionary.thefreedictionary.com.

Lowe, Jamie. *Ten Sessions.* This American Life. August 26, 2019.

McLeod, Saul. *Erik Erikson's Stages of Psychosocial Development.* Simply Psychology. updated 2018.

Rape, Abuse and Incest National Network. https://www.rainn.org.

Rottweil, Meg. Bessel van der Kolk podcast: "How to Detoxify the Body from Trauma," Youtube. May 26, 2016.

The Science of Success. Bessel van der Kolk podcast: "Healing Trauma: How to Start Feeling Safe in your Own Body," Youtube. April 19, 2019.

Sexual Assault Support Services of Midcoast Maine. https:// www.sassmm.org.

Sujata, K. *Sexual Assault in the Age of Social Media.* The Huffington Post. October 6, 2016.

Waack, Terrin. *As a College Student, I Live in Fear of Sexual Assault.* Sporting News. June 8, 2016.

The Woman Who Created #MeToo Long Before Hashtags. The New York Times. October, 20, 2017.

CPSIA information can be obtained
at www.ICGtesting.com
Printed in the USA
LVHW091617221021
701206LV00009B/1003